Force Drawing Human Anatomy

Force Drawing Human Anatomy

Michael Mattesi

CRC Press
Taylor & Francis Group
Boca Raton London New York

CRC Press is an imprint of the
Taylor & Francis Group, an **informa** business

A FOCAL PRESS BOOK

CRC Press
Taylor & Francis Group
6000 Broken Sound Parkway NW, Suite 300
Boca Raton, FL 33487-2742

Printed on acid-free paper
Version Date: 20161114

International Standard Book Number-13: 978-0-4157-3397-7 (Paperback); 978-1-1387-3123-3 (Hardback)

Library of Congress Cataloging-in-Publication Data

Names: Mattesi, Michael D., author
Title: Force. Drawing human anatomy / Michael Mattesi.
Other titles: Drawing human anatomy
Description: Boca Raton : CRC Press, 2016. | Includes index.
Identifiers: LCCN 2016032408| ISBN 9780415733977 (pbk. : alk. paper) | ISBN 9781138731233 (hardback : alk. paper)
Subjects: LCSH: Anatomy, Artistic. | Figure drawing--Technique.
Classification: LCC NC760 .M425 2016 | DDC 743.4--dc23
LC record available at https://lccn.loc.gov/2016032408

Visit the Taylor & Francis Web site at
http://www.taylorandfrancis.com

and the CRC Press Web site at
http://www.crcpress.com

This book is dedicated to the models who have inspired my students and me to experience the beauty and strength of the human body.

Contents

Special Thanks

In any endeavor, there are many great people behind the scenes that share in a vision and allow it to become reality. First and foremost there is my family: my ever-supportive wife Ellen and inspiring daughters Marin and Makenna. They consistently encourage me to follow my dreams and aspirations.

To the Focal Press team: Katy Spencer, my first editor on this book; Haley Swan, the second editor, who carried me through the last two-thirds of this book; and finally Sean Connelly, executive editor, who brought me and this book over the finish line. Thank you all for your support. A thank you as well to the production team, Jessica Vega at CRC and Adel Rosario, the project manager for this book.

To Stephen Busfield, my sounding board, thank you for your great insight, candid commentary, and edits!

Mike Mattesi

Preface

Hundreds of years ago, during the 1500s in Italy, the Renaissance exploded. This period in art created some of the most notable artists, "Renaissance men" such as Michelangelo and Leonardo Da Vinci, who created much of the world's most exquisite art. Much of this art is considered "studies." That's right; they drew to study the figure, not to create beautiful drawings. The drawings were by-products of curious and inspired minds.

It is your **curiosity** that I call forth as we investigate human anatomy. I propose using the drawing language of FORCE as a vehicle to understand how the human body functions, not for the sake of learning how to draw. Your humility to humanity can incite your hunger to become an amazing artist! The human body is both intellectually complex and lyrically poetic.

All of the human body's systems, including the muscular system, are designed based on FORCES. These FORCES drive the numerous functions of this amazing and complex machine. This machine contains many smaller machines of different types: pulley systems, levers, torque, and an endless amount of inventions that we interact with today are inspired by the mechanics observed in the human machine. George Bridgeman, in fact, compared the different areas of the body to these types of mechanisms in his classic "how-to-draw" book, *Constructive Anatomy* (1966).

I learn by taking complex ideas and simplifying them down to their bare components. I need to know the basics in order to understand the intricate. Therefore, I have worked hard at clarifying the mysteries and complexities of the human body. This work started with how to structure this book. What is the best way to present the knowledge? It took almost a year to figure out the setup you hold in your hands today. I color-coded the anatomical regions of the figure based on their collective, FORCEFUL functions. Each region presents three sides of rotation so you can see the anatomy from all directions. To constantly remind us of how each area ties into the bigger picture through the rhythms of the figure, I added FORCE figure drawings to each chapter that have the region's anatomy appropriately color coded.

FORCE is the answer and foundation to anatomy.

Where is a muscle located, and why is it there?

I want you, the reader, the artist, to understand that, when I experience drawing the figure, there are hidden filters I use in my decision-making process. Within each chapter, I discuss those filters, FORCE, form, shape, and then the specific anatomy of that region.

I will share with you the secrets I have learned from the thousands of drawings I have experienced. The body functions in specific ways. There are FORCE rules in place due to the body's anatomy. In time, you will learn how anatomy is drawn and defined by the **function** of a pose. **I draw the functions, and the anatomy appears, not the other way around. If you draw a deltoid, you get a deltoid. If you draw the thrust into the deltoid, then you will draw that thrust, and therefore the deltoid muscle will be drawn. This difference in thinking is essential to the FORCE drawing experience.**

The process I am sharing can help you if you are a hobbyist, an animator, a comic book artist, a concept artist, or a three-dimensional modeler, among many other art disciplines. So, in the spirit of the Renaissance, let us embark on our journey to understand the FORCEFUL function of the human body's anatomy and, at the same time, be amazed by its beauty!

Key Concepts

THE TRUTH IS OUT THERE!

There is something that I want to be real clear about here at the beginning of the book. FORCE is not a concept that I am asking you to apply to the figure; FORCE already exists! I am sharing it with you, doing my best to help you see it in the world and experience it through the act of drawing! To some people, it is obvious and easy to witness; all they need is a frame of reference. To others, it takes more time and physical drawing practice to acknowledge and admire its existence.

HIERARCHY

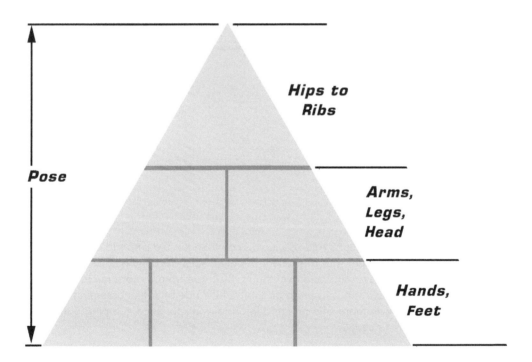

All of my other FORCE books discuss hierarchy because it is integral to understanding, drawing, and experiencing the FORCES of the human body. This FORCE anatomy book is no exception. Thinking hierarchically, or from big to small, is a profound method to assessing challenges. When drawing the human body, the whole pyramid represents the main idea of the pose or moment. The biggest ideas in the figure are at the top of the pyramid such as the relationship between the rib cage and the pelvis. As we move down the tiers of the pyramid, the rhythms decrease in size until we observe fingers and toes. Hierarchy creates a clearly defined path and priorities that then assist in the comprehension of complex ideas. Human nature seems to initially resist this idea. We want to get mired in the details instead of seeing the big picture. Hierarchy is so profound that you can use it on anything, not just your drawing experience. It could be used in work procedures, to organize your process for food shopping, the flow of automotive traffic, personal relationships, and more.

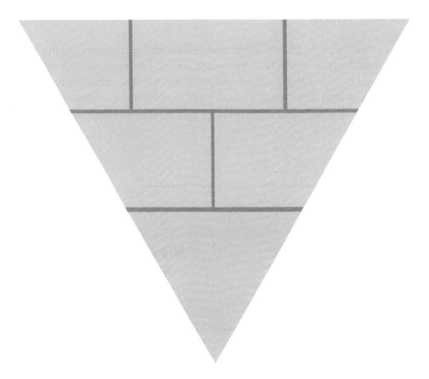

After truly and fully comprehending how to use it, you can then flip the pyramid on its head. What does this mean? You can now start with a moment of detail, such as the finger, because you first have understood the big picture. Now, you can travel the FORCE ride from a more micro-level experience. A very exciting process to draw with is to jump on the FORCE ride after first assessing the big picture. Then, you ride the coaster with more of a rich and informative experience, jumping out of the micro view to see the macro when needed.

FEAR

I have taught at Pixar, Walt Disney, and DreamWorks, numerous art schools, and video game companies, and I am here to say that, whether you are a professional or not, there is still fear to conquer! Fear is the most detrimental blockade to the pursuit of knowledge. Fear comes in all forms, some more obvious than others. The top reasons for fear I have witnessed from students and myself are as follows:

1. Fear based on perfection. "My drawing has to be perfect. If it is not, then I have failed, and thus I am a failure."

2. Fear of the teacher. "I hope I am doing the right thing."

3. Fear of judgment. "I don't want others thinking I am stupid."

"The greatest barrier to success is the fear of failure."
Sven Goran Erikkson

INTERNAL DIALOGUE

Use it to help you, not hurt you. Notice when and why you are indecisive or concerned. Allow drawing to be about your experience and curiosity, not the final product. Remember the Renaissance! We are drawing to learn/study, not to draw pretty pictures. YOU create the fear, so rid yourself of it! It will only slow you down. Remember, you are drawing, not jumping out of airplanes, shark hunting, or living in the Great Depression, so fear nothing!

Your mind-set is essential to this dialogue. Stay curious and hungry to learn. Experience the 10,000 hours of drawing and learning that give you the sense of accomplishment that comes with practice! Do NOT judge yourself, but instead learn from your experiences to improve. The act of writing this book has taught me a great deal about the anatomy of the human body!

RISK

In order to grow, you must take risk, or what you perceive as risk. A risk to one individual is the norm to another. Be aware of that. Use your curiosity and passion for learning to push through your risks. This is where your courage and pride will come from. In order to have an opinion, you MUST be able to take risk! You MUST move beyond your fears. You MUST be willing to fall flat on your face to pursue your creativity and become more than who you are today! Once you break the bonds of fear and love feeling risk while you work, you will never turn back.

THE POWER OF QUESTIONS

When you stare at the white paper and then back at the model and start thinking—"I don't know what to do!"—it is time to control your thoughts and shift your focus to the power of questions. The question that got me out of doubt and turmoil is "What do I want?" This very powerful question forces your mind into creating answers. "I want to find the largest FORCE and experience it! I want to see shape and design in the figure. I want to learn how to draw **Human Anatomy with FORCE!**"

OPINION

Strengthening your ability to take greater and greater risks allows you to get out of the "kind-of" mind-set. New students look at life and "kind of" see it. You must see truth in order to form an opinion. Opinions come from heightened clarity! Much of this clarity comes from knowledge. Your search for knowledge comes from curiosity. Don't draw with mediocrity; strive for opinion through clarity. What are you trying to say? How do you feel during your experience of drawing the subject? The act of drawing many hours alone without some real thought might get you some muscle memory, but you must observe yourself and your work to improve upon both.

Use creative ideas when drawing human anatomy with FORCE. You might have a thought that is an analogy. Perhaps, the figure's pose reminds you of a natural power, architecture, culture, a time period, a character, an automobile, or a famous artist's work. Draw upon your intuition to inspire your experience.

ENVISION AND EMPOWERMENT

When I attended art school, I would play games with my mind. I would look at the model and then envision my drawing on the page. My image of my drawing was far beyond my abilities at that time, but I do believe that the repetition of this activity allowed me to believe in myself and attain my goals more quickly. It is empowering to ask yourself if you are doing your best and answering honestly. You are capable of more than what you are achieving. Hold yourself to excellence. I promise you that you will be amazed by your true potential!

When you look down at your drawing, and it is not what you envisioned, that is great! Notice the differences between the envisioned and the reality. Now, you know what you need to work on, and you can set goals to go after! It may be that you notice your drawing does not have enough FORCE and anatomy, and that is why you are reading this book!

CONTRAST AND AFFINITY

While working at Walt Disney Feature Animation, one of the best rules I learned was "CONTRAST CREATES INTEREST." Beware of mediocrity through the lack of contrast. Look for idiosyncrasies, asymmetry, unparalleled moments, and varied lines. This rule works for character design, landscape painting, film editing, writing, and all artistic works. Contrast is self-explanatory, but how many ideas can be contrasted? That is where the magic happens. A line on a piece of paper can have much contrast or little contrast. Is the line parallel to the edges of the paper, or is it at a 45° angle? Is there variety in the weight of the line? How long or short is the line? Does it go off of the page? When drawing the human figure, we think we all look alike…we all have two arms, legs, eyes, and so on. The real magic happens when you see the idiosyncratic nuances: "Wow, this model's elbows are larger than mine, her hip is long and thin, he has a heavy brow."

All of these possibilities represent different ideas in the world of art. Remember that every mark on the page has meaning: a meaning to create the bigger purpose of the artist's statement!

Affinity or unity means the similarity between items in the drawings. This gives you another opportunity for contrast…the contrast between contrast and affinity.

Design is an abstract way of looking at our world and using it to communicate our thoughts. Your art is only as powerful as your thoughts and how you communicate them with your skills. I hope to present you with some new tools to assist you in communicating your experiences.

IN THE ZONE, FLOW, PRESENCE

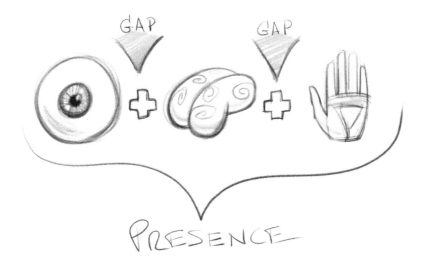

During the act of drawing, we move through three steps: (1) seeing, (2) thinking about what we see, and then (3) using our hand to draw it. The issues that occur with this process are in the gaps between the steps. Typically, we look at something, and then our minds create their own version of what we saw. Then, we draw THAT idea. Closing this first gap between the eye and the mind is crucial. Your mind needs to believe what it actually sees. Try drawing without looking at the page. Then, to close the second gap, focus on your hand moving at the speed your eye sees and your mind thinks. So become a FORCE drawing addict, and feel the power of drawing in FLOW!

A current focus in our world is the concept of flow, which is the state you get into where all focus is on the task at hand, where time either speeds up or slows down, and your mind is like a laser. This is the same idea that has existed for centuries within Buddhism. The act of drawing is a perfect vehicle for experiencing flow. In fact, in my 20+ years of teaching, I have always said that this state is the goal we are after, and, once reached, it is like an addiction. I just found out that science proves that many of the body's natural, "feel-good" chemicals are released into the body when in a state of flow.

THE KEY TO MUSCULAR FUNCTION

The human body functions due to the **CONTRACTION** of muscles. When one side of the figure contracts, the other side **STRETCHES**. I will use these two terms throughout the book to describe the function of the muscles.

RESISTANCE

As I just described, when a muscle contracts, it shortens and typically brings two bones closer together. Anything that opposes this action is a resistance FORCE. Gravity is a constant resistance, but a resistance FORCE could be something else, such as a rubber band, or another individual.

Sometimes, the resistance comes in the form of slowing down another muscle's CONTRACTION combined with gravity, such as bending over. Your abs help you bend over, but the muscles in your back also slightly contract to slow down the fall of your upper body.

SUPPLIES

Most of the drawings in this book were created with soft graphite. Some drawings, including the male template drawing, were drawn in my favorite drawing program, Made with Mischief. Last and definitely not the least, some images were drawn in faithful work horse, Photoshop, with a Wacom Cintiq, where all the color work was also accomplished.

So let's get started: how to draw and experience FORCE.

Chapter 1
The Power of FORCE

FORCE is a challenging topic to teach. It is far less obvious to witness than measurement and proportion. Those topics are also, at times, difficult to instruct since they demand the visual clarity of the artist for the awareness to occur. FORCE is invisible. It is not tattooed on the body. I have experienced over the years that FORCE is more quickly understood if, at first, the artist draws striving for the FORCE "experience." Drawing with the line that I will present to you conveys a physical activity. You must "feel" FORCE running through the figure by mimicking and understanding rhythmic FORCES in the body. In the first few chapters, I will cover the basics of FORCE. For a deeper understanding of the theory, read *FORCE: Dynamic Life Drawing*, 10th Anniversary Edition (2017).

This anniversary edition of FORCE has video tutorials that present what the FORCE experience of drawing looks like as you see me create them.

At the time of publication of this book, I have been teaching drawing for 26 years. In those years I experimented alongside the students I taught on what types of marks work best for FORCE and why. I observed and became aware of students' habits when they entered my classes and investigated why they had those habits and how to change them. Some students changed quickly, others took much longer…some never changed or grew at all.

If you are an instructor using this book for your class, don't judge. In my early years of teaching, I would have my own thoughts on who I thought would excel quickly and who would never get it early in a term, and at times I was extremely surprised by the students' results. Stay open to each student; inspire them to learn! You will be amazed at who can take off like a rocket with a bit of focus and encouragement.

Since we are DRAWING to learn, we need to use a line. The image above presents two types of drawing approaches shown in black that I see commonly used. The black lines in the left example come from a fear of drawing. The concern to get it right, committing, and being accurate stifle the artist. The sketchy, black line example on the right is the opposite approach. A more careless attitude is taken; a lack of responsibility to the model comes into play…or does it? Sometimes, this artist is actually the artist on the left in disguise, and is so terrified to draw that the fear is overwhelming, so they resort to the careless approach.

This is it, folks, **THE FORCE line**! Everything in this book and all my other books is built on this stroke because the stroke itself represents the **IDEA of FORCE**. It appears to be so simple and inconspicuous, yet it is so powerful. Let's look at it more closely. Notice the following:

1. It tapers at the beginning and end of the stroke. What does that mean? I drew it while my hand was in motion.

2. The line is thicker at its apex. I pressed hardest at that moment in time, not before or after that moment.

Let me share with you the thoughts that occur for me while drawing this amazing line. The FORCE line above is called a DIRECTIONAL FORCE line.

It has three components:

1. Coming from…

2. Main event/apex

3. Going to…

As I mentioned prior, the line is an idea, FORCE. Within that idea are the three components you will think about while drawing it. The blue color you see above is the color I will use throughout the rest of the book to present Directional FORCE.

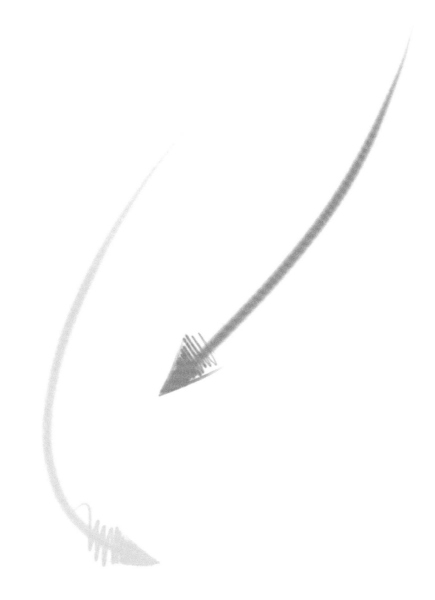

There is a second FORCE you need to think about when drawing a Directional FORCE, and that is APPLIED FORCE. It will always be represented by this orange color. This second FORCE pushes upon the Directional FORCE at its apex, causing the amount of curvature to appear. Where did this Applied FORCE come from?

Applied FORCE is the mass of the body pushing against the edge of the form that you see at that specific moment in time. Above are varied examples of Applied FORCE presenting different amounts of Applied FORCE.

Applied FORCE is a **prior** Directional FORCE applying itself to the Directional FORCE you are drawing at the moment. This can be seen with the orange arrow connecting the two Directional FORCES. Once you have two Directional FORCES and one Applied FORCE connecting them, you have one rhythm.

Rhythm creates balance. The human figure is not only made of FORCE but also form, otherwise known as anatomy. The top-left image presents a balanced, vertical line since the sphere at the top is perfectly centered on the vertical axis. The center image shows how a form, the hemisphere, when on one side of the vertical blue line, wants to fall to the left side. The downward blue arrow shows how gravity would pull the hemisphere down in an arc toward the ground. The bottom-right image offsets the hemispheres, retaining balance yet creating rhythm!

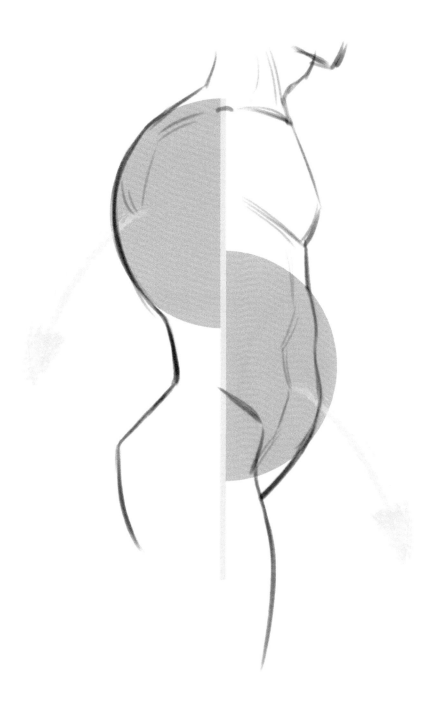

Here is the abstract of form on our centerline of balance superimposed with a figure drawing. See how the upper back balances with the abdomen.

When you define more than one mass on only one side of the centerline of balance, the figure is immediately out of balance. If the time period to draw was over at this time, the drawing would be out of balance. I call this issue the "bunny hop" since you end up with a double bounce or a hop. As soon as you see one FORCE, know it will lead you across the figure to create balance.

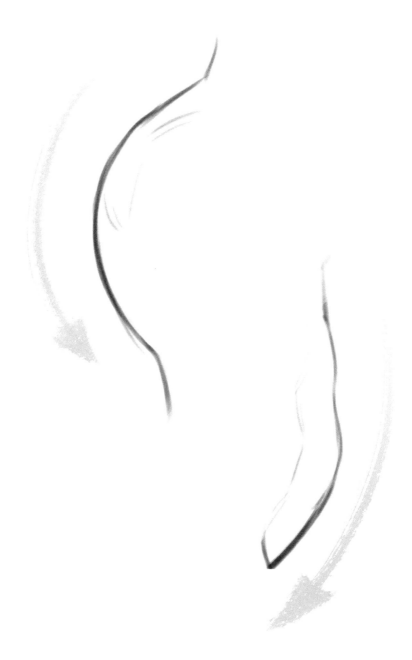

Here is the figure without the mass shapes. See how connecting the first two FORCES immediately create balance and rhythm! It is the relationship between these two Directional FORCES that creates a rhythm.

PROFILE VIEW TEMPLATE

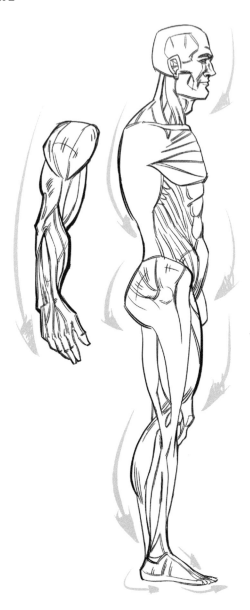

Above is a rhythm template of the figure in profile. See how FORCE bounces from side to side across the centerline of balance.

These distances and regions of the FORCE rhythms determine the anatomical breakdown of the book's chapters.

FRONT VIEW TEMPLATE

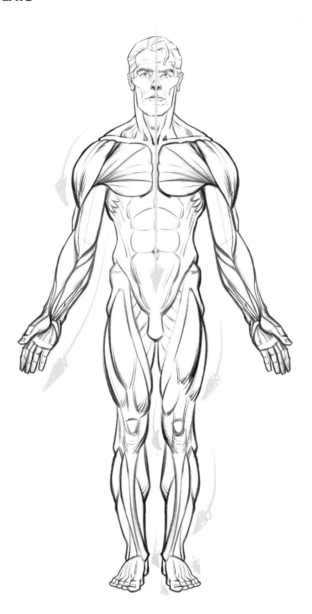

Here is the template for the front of the figure. You will notice that most of the upper body is symmetrical. It is in the limbs that we find some rhythm. This is due to the function of the muscles. In the upper body, all of the opposing muscles' functions of the figure are mostly found in the relationships between the front and back muscles of the body. That is why, in the side view, we find much rhythm. The rear view of the figure contains the same rhythms as the front.

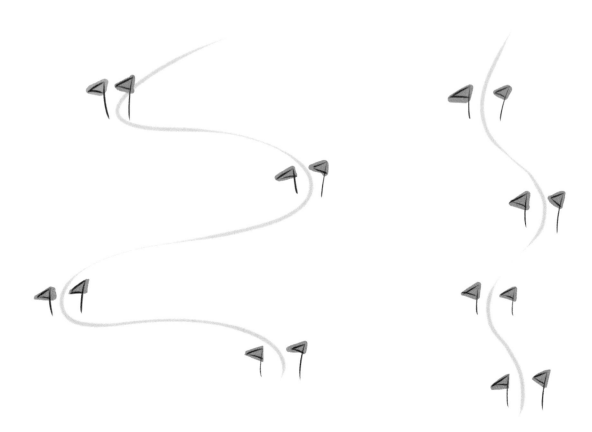

One analogy I often use to understand the feeling or experience of drawing with FORCE is skiing. Gravity pulls you down the mountain. Your body wants to slide in a straight line down to the bottom, but you angle your skis to the side, and you change your body's trajectory. This causes a lot of FORCE on the downhill side of your skis. Once you travel to the edge of the trail, you push or jump into the new trajectory, pointed toward the other side of the slope. Bouncing and sliding back and forth down the slippery, snow-covered surface of the mountain is similar to the drawing experience of FORCE.

The drawings above present the difference in speed of traveling down the mountain relative to the change in the trajectory's angle from one side of the trail to another. A stronger angle change, more acute, takes you on a more perpendicular path across the mountain, thus slowing you down. The image on the right shows an obtuse angle change, thus moving you more parallel to the slope of the mountain. Doing this increases your speed through the figure.

CONTRACTION

This book introduces a NEW FORCE, **CONTRACTION! The muscles of the human body contract or shorten over the span of a joint, and that is how they function**. For instance, if you want to lift your hand to your face, you contract your bicep. The bicep moves over the elbow joint; therefore, shortening those muscles lifts the forearm upward.

In this image of numerous colored arrows, I have added GREEN to represent **CONTRACTION**. You can see how Directional FORCE moves across to the stretched side and then returns to the right side below the contracted area.

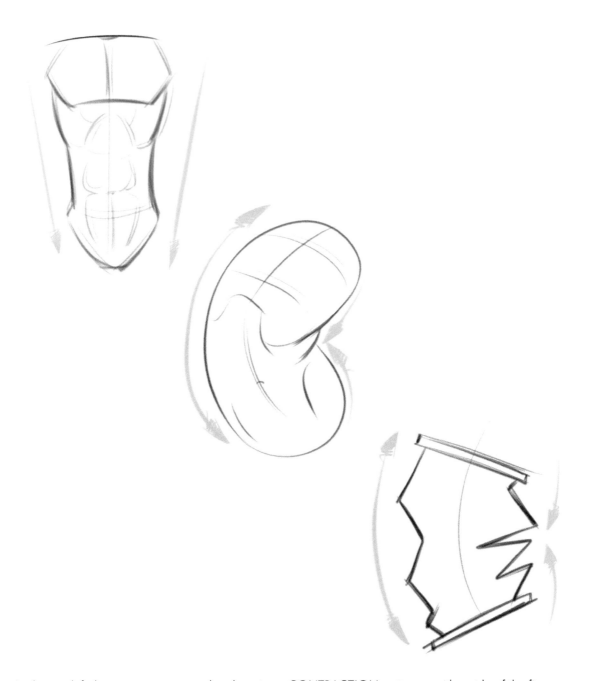

In the top-left drawing, you can see that there is no CONTRACTION action on either side of the figure, but, as soon as CONTRACTION occurs, FORCE can be seen on the opposing side. The bottom-right drawing shows an accordion, a simple example of how the bending occurs between the rib cage and the hips. As one side contracts, the other side stretches.

This drawing is created by purely experiencing FORCE! The lines evoke the expression of the body's power and connectivity. Directional, Applied, and CONTRACTION FORCES come together to move the masses of the figure. We are drawing the HOW and not the WHAT, or the VERB, not the NOUN.

Anatomy is barely described at this stage.

With the major FORCES called out, you can witness the poetry of the body in motion. The forward thrust in the pelvis drives this figure forward. The leftward drive of the upper body brings us up into the deltoid, which then allows us to flow down the arms.

Here are a few more one-minute poses. See how FORCE, anatomy, and shape come together to create a quick, informative gesture drawing. You can now see the pectorals, scapula, ankles, and more. See if you can locate the Directional, Applied, and CONTRACTION FORCE in the drawings.

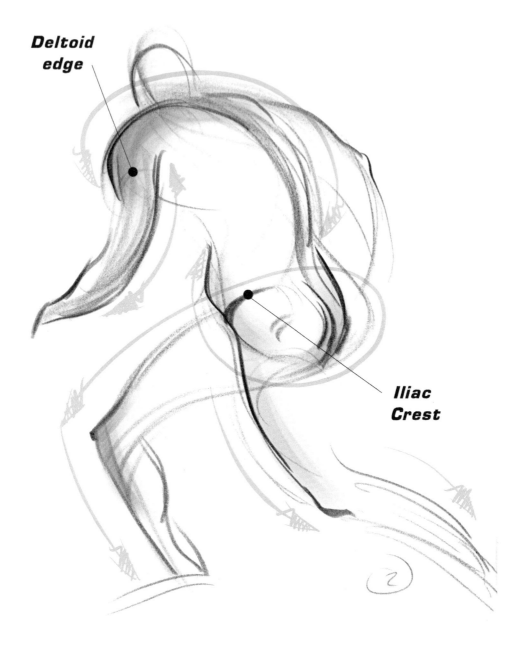

Deltoid edge

Iliac Crest

The above two-minute drawing clearly presents the flow or rhythm of FORCE through the entire figure from hand to foot. Again, some subtle anatomy is seen here to present form. Look at the light looping line that suggests the deltoid and the iliac crest. Of course, the spine helps set up the structure of the back.

There are anatomical rules that dictate how these rhythms glide through the figure. It is these rules that we will uncover in the upcoming pages of this book. An understanding of anatomy allows you to draw it with efficiency in shorter periods of time.

EXERCISES AND TIPS

1. Try to ski the figure and feel what it is like to draw with FORCE!

2. Draw FORCE without looking at the page, but instead focus on the model. Use FORCE as the pathway around the body.

3. Draw softly/gently, and then become more loud. Build up your confidence.

4. Practice the FORCE line over and over again. Draw one line over and over again, then allow the thought of "Where does this go next?" Apply FORCE to the next directional.

Chapter 2
Mass and FORCEFUL Form

Form is anatomy when it comes to the human figure. How can we show form with lines? Form is somewhat invisible to the untrained eye. We can see a ball or a cube, but can we place lines on those forms to describe their surfaces?

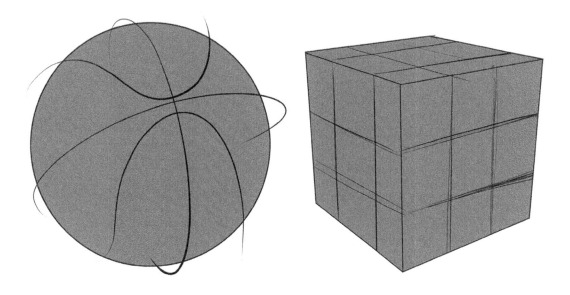

When you look at a basketball, you can see the lines wrap around the ball. When you look at a Rubik's Cube, you can see the lines that define the separations of the numerous smaller cubes. These obvious lines are what you must perceive on the human body when there are no lines to see.

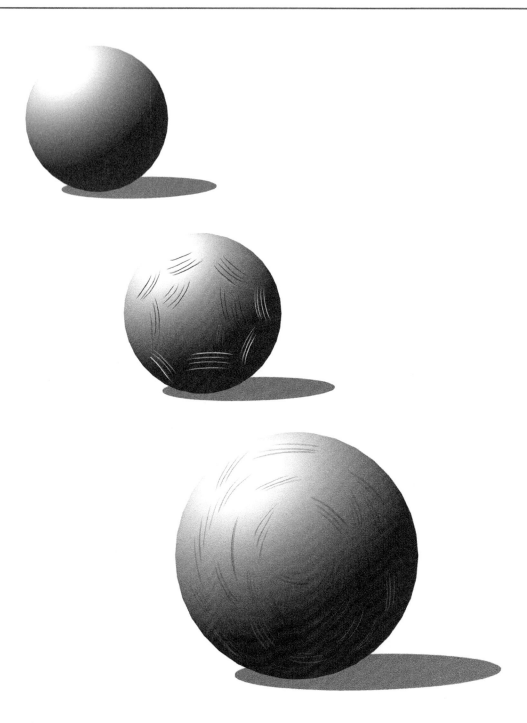

We see form as light and shadow, created by changes in tone, from light to dark. We need to transfer this impression of form in terms of a line. The center sphere shows the line going against the surface of the sphere's form. The bottom sphere presents lines that adhere to the form.

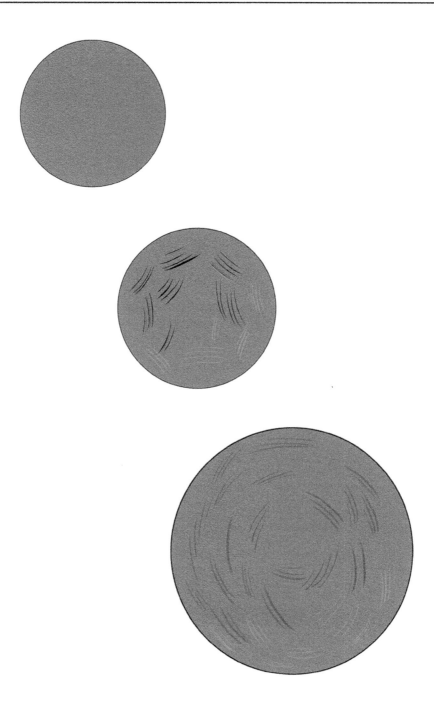

Let's take the sphere and flatten it out to a circle. This removes the changes in tone and thus any sense of form. Again, the center circle shows lines that do not support form within the flat, circular shape. In fact, it looks like we could travel into the center of the circle, the opposite of what the sphere does, which is to push out toward us at the center. The bottom circle is filled with the lines that create form.

Finally, here is our circle without the assistance of tonal changes. The lines alone define form within the circle.

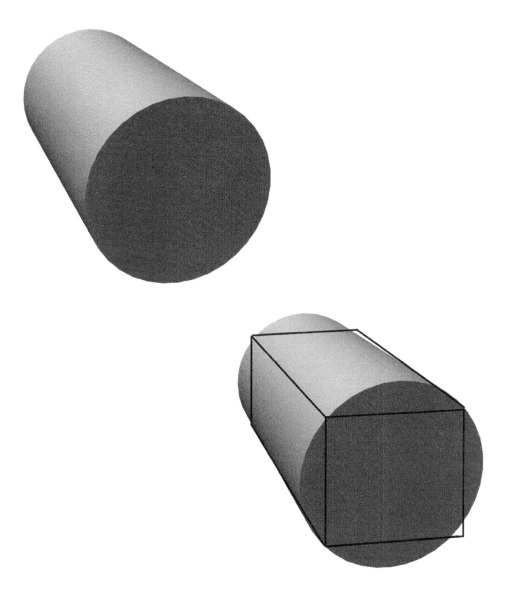

When drawing the human figure, we see many of its forms as tubes, especially the limbs. The difficulty around the tube form is that its surface is unclear, so, to better understand it, I propose finding the right angles within the tube. Once you understand the structural clarity and orientation of the form with more right angles, we can then address sculpting the tube more accurately with a surface line. As you can see above, the top-left corner image presents a tube. The bottom-right image presents an internal, right-angled structure.

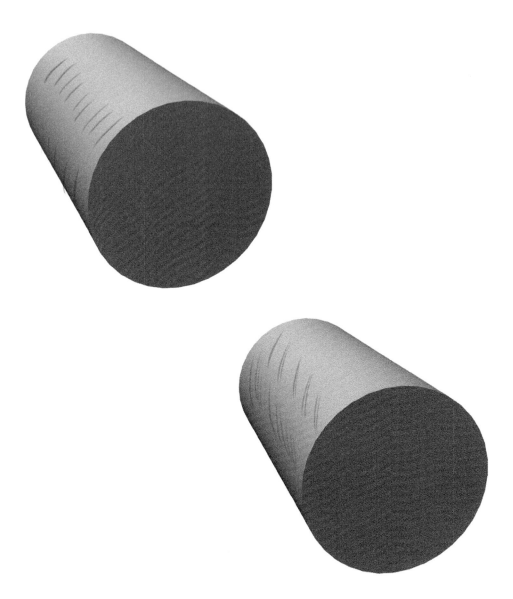

The top-left tube shows surface lines perpendicular to the orientation of the form. This method to defining form creates great solidity, but any sense of FORCE is destroyed. The solution is therefore found in the bottom-right tube. The FORCEFUL surface lines still adhere to the tube's form, but they are angled along the surface to present a FORCE direction.

I don't like turning the figure into tubes and boxes though. That is why I use the surface line and edges to define simple structures or more specific anatomy. A great way to do this is to add a basic NONFORCEFUL surface line at the beginning or end of a long form, such as the forearm. Here, there are NONFORCEFUL surface lines that are near the elbow and the wrist. Clarifying the form in these locations allows the mind to fill in the rest of the form and anatomy. Then, I can determine if I want to add more detailed information describing anatomy.

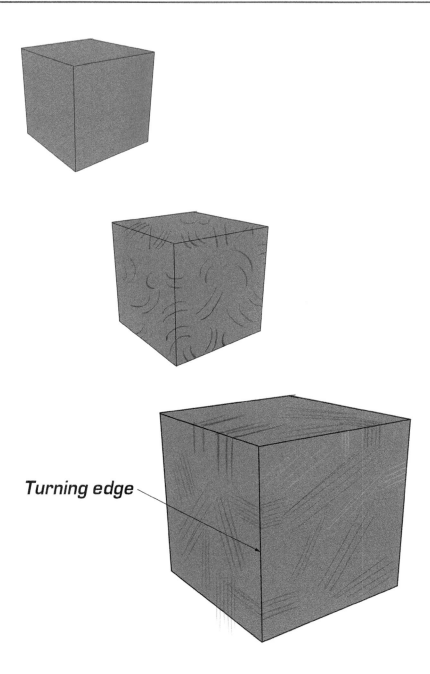

Turning edge

Following the same process, let's look at the ever-important cube. Since the surfaces are flat, gradations are not as needed as on the sphere. The center cube presents lines that defeat the structure of the cube's surfaces and, most importantly, its hard edges. The cube at the bottom has structurally supportive lines. See how they adhere to surfaces and turn around the edges of the cube. The vertical edge closest to us is what I like to call the **TURNING EDGE**. This is where form turns from surface to another on the cube.

Here is the cube with only surface line support. See how the lines help inform us of the cube's surfaces and edges without turning edges.

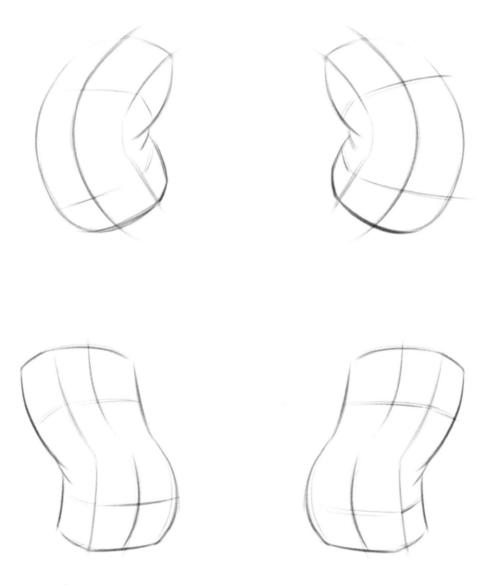

Now, when we see the shape filled with lines, we can describe form. The red lines present the NATURAL CENTERS, and the green lines present the TURNING EDGES. Natural centers are exactly what the term refers to: centers that are natural on the human figure. Some examples would be the sternum, the belly button, elbows, kneecaps, and more. I will point to more of these natural centers throughout the book to assist in your understanding of structure.

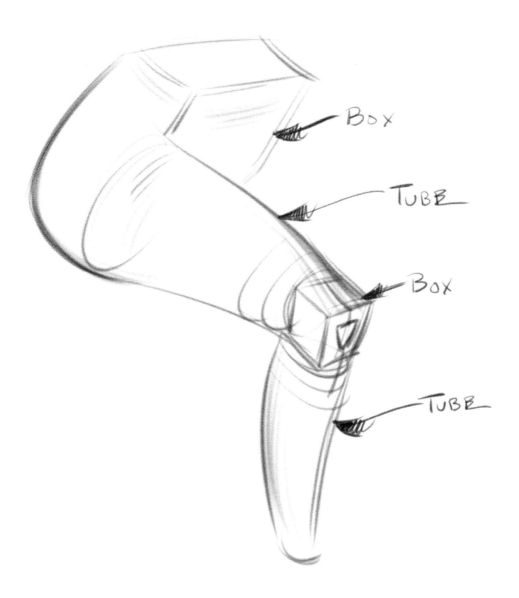

It is through the combination of these simple forms that we can understand the complexities of the figure. Notice how the kneecap helps set the orientation of the structure of the leg. The results I see artists fall into through only drawing tubes and boxes are unforceful drawings. Remember that FORCE is the foundation to the function and vitality of the figure. So, to be clear, know the forms but do not draw for the sake of form. FORCE is the primary purpose behind the experience of drawing the figure.

Above, I have also added a few surface lines. Let's take these surface lines to a more complex structure, the skull!

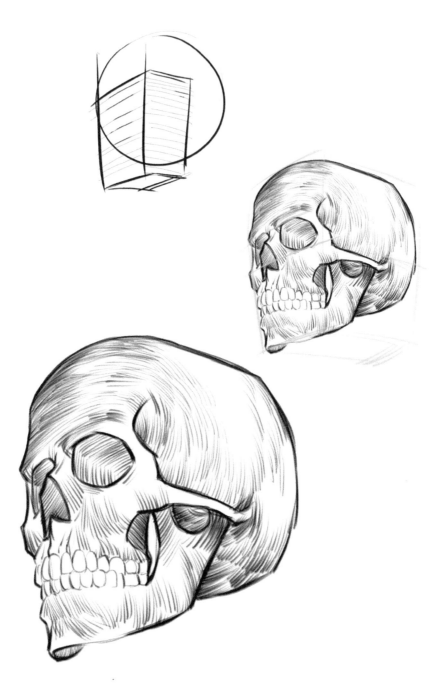

These skull drawings present the combination of different, simple geometric forms. In the top-left corner, you can see the combination of the sphere and the box. The complexity is found in the variation across the surfaces. To observe with this level of clarity requires understanding the abstract of the geometry and owning a high clarity of sight.

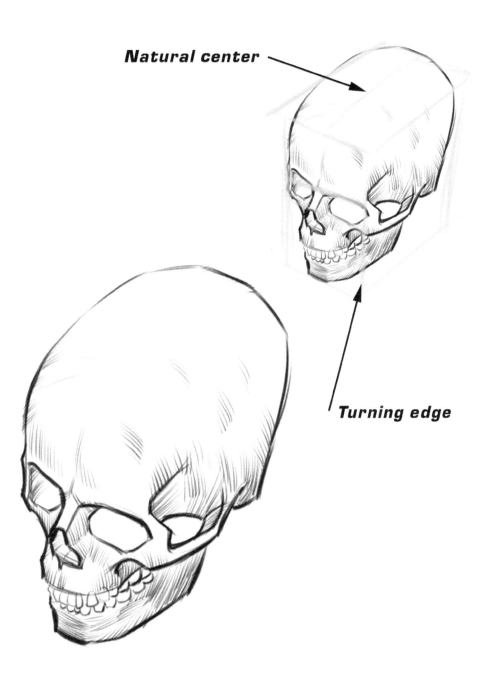

Natural center

Turning edge

In angles as dramatic as this one, the cube becomes even more important. Since the skull is a rigid structure, I find one angle in the face that I can clearly see and understand, such as the angle created across the eyes. That angled line is my ladder for the rest of the face. Whatever the angle of the eyes, the same angle goes for the nose, the chin, and the top of the forehead, as presented with the blue lines.

EXERCISES AND TIPS

1. Practice placing a line on the surface of forms.

    a. Try sculpting a skull or a wrinkled fabric.

2. Learn the one- to four-point perspective, further defined in *FORCE: Dynamic Life Drawing,* 10th Anniversary Edition (2017).

3. Learn to see the turning edge and the natural centers.

4. Combine the ideas in numbers 1 through 3.

5. Draw numerous cubes without any extension lines.

Chapter 3
FORCE Shape

INTRODUCTION

Seeing the world through the filter of shapes imbued with FORCE is a method to simplifying the intense amount of anatomical information we typically see. The challenge lies in understanding how to create these simplifications. When created incorrectly, the body's shapes from the entire figure's silhouette to the shape of a muscle can become cumbersome and lack cohesive fluidity.

Master illustrators, animation companies, and many successful artists use certain tricks to make their work appealing. What does appealing mean? After all, appeal is subjective. I mean shapes that create rhythm in the figure and therefore lack a sense of awkwardness or make the body look broken.

What I share with you in this chapter on shape are the simple tricks to solving this ever difficult problem, how to keep your anatomical drawings full of FORCE and rhythm. Believe it or not, there are rules to clarify what works and what does not.

THE RULES OF FORCE SHAPE

There are dead shapes and live shapes, or FORCEFUL and NONFORCEFUL shapes. The top three shapes represent the dead. The reason I call them dead is that they have no clear direction. This is due to their symmetry.

The bottom three shapes are the FORCEFUL versions. They now all have clear direction...they all push toward the top right. The blue arrow shows the DIRECTIONAL FORCE of each shape. The orange color shows the region with the most APPLIED FORCE for each shape...the leading edge. Leading edge can be brought over to a three-dimensional space and thought more of as a leading surface.

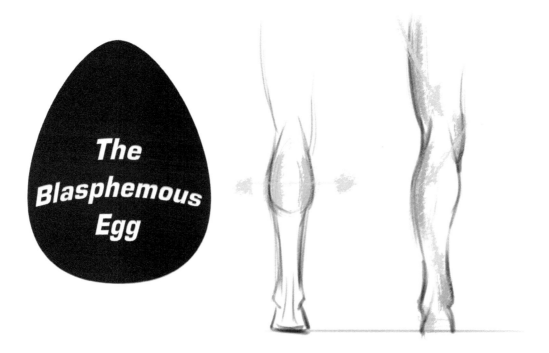

One of the most commonly used shapes I see used in drawing instruction is what I call the "blasphemous egg." The reason it is blasphemous is that there are no egg-shaped muscles in the figure, AND the egg is a symmetrical shape. A common area of the figure I see this form used for is the calf, as seen in the back of the left legs drawn above. The image on the left shows the egg used and how it creates a FORCELESS blockage in the lower leg. The image to the right is designed around the real shape of the calf and how its asymmetry allows FORCE to flow through the leg down to the foot.

Do Not Draw Ellipses

The ellipse is as detrimental a culprit in killing FORCE as the egg, due to the fact that both shapes are symmetrical. In addition, the muscles of the body do not exist in this shape. So, if you see this elliptical concept in a book or a Website, ignore it. I understand that it is used to describe a simple form, but that is where the issue lies. The form then takes precedence over function, the main error in figure drawing instruction.

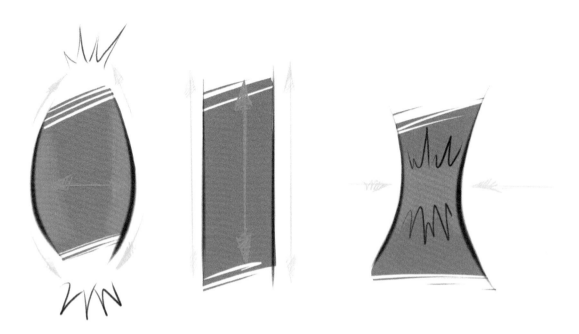

Above are more DON'TS of shape! They are all symmetrical. This symmetry prevents them from allowing FORCE to move from shape to shape.

Left: Applied FORCE pushes out equally on both sides of the shape, and the Directional FORCES crash at the top and bottom of what I call the candy or sausage shape.

Center: This shape is similar to a pipe, lacking asymmetry and thus any way for FORCE to bounce to the next shape.

Right: Directional FORCES squeeze symmetrically into the center of this shape, once more closing the opportunity for asymmetry and thus FORCE moving from one shape to the next.

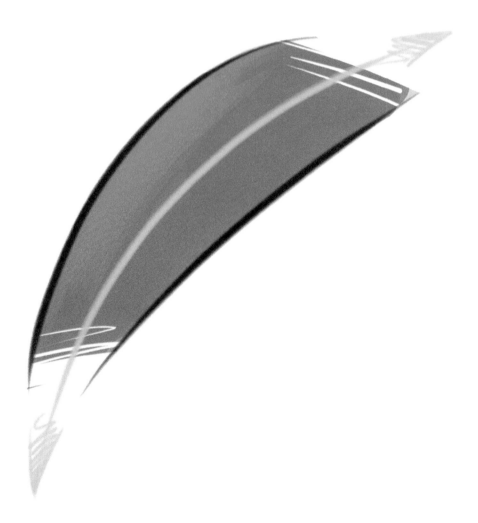

Above is our FORCE SHAPE, very similar to that of an arrow. The curve represents FORCE, the straight is structure. FORCE can move through this shape due to the asymmetry. This shape is malleable. As we move through the book, I will call out how to see the core simple shapes of the body and then how to sculpt them to more accurate shapes that represent the true anatomical forms of the body.

Let's take this shape theory to our smallest common denominator for this book: a muscle.

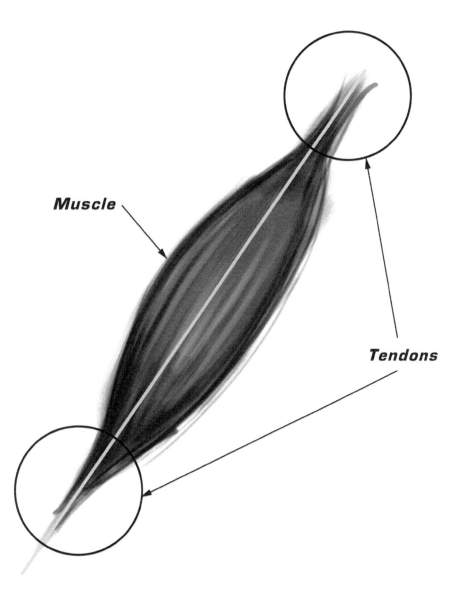

Muscle

Tendons

In this muscle, we can see how easy it is to fall into the trap of symmetry. Above is a muscle with its accompanying tendons. Tendons are the ends of the muscle that are attached to the bone.

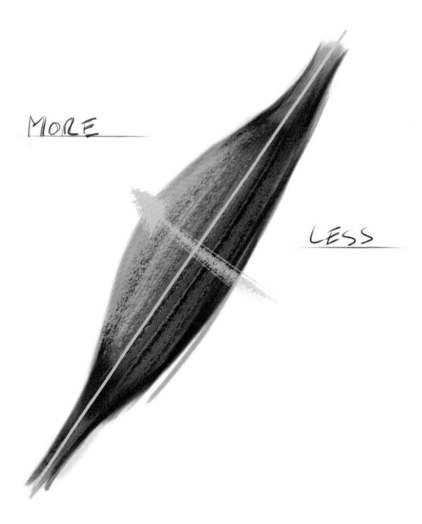

MORE

LESS

We want to apply asymmetry to the muscle. So, above, you can see that the left side of the muscle now has more mass than the right. The problem here is that, although we have solved the issue of asymmetry on the blue-lined axis, we still have symmetry along the angle where the blue arrow is. FORCE now pushes right through the center of the shape.

Here is the last iteration. Now, we have moved away from the vertical symmetry and the horizontal symmetry. FORCE now has a clear direction; here it is thrusting to the top-left corner.

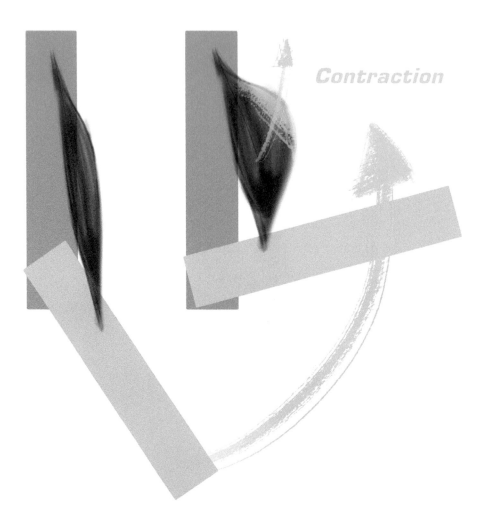

Above is a sample of a stretched and then contracted muscle, a little squash and stretch for you. With every book I write, I learn a great deal myself. One such epiphany was that all of the figure's amazing functions are possible due to the simple function of MUSCULAR CONTRACTIONS. CONTRACTION, or the shortening of the muscle, is what moves our bones around, creating motion with purpose.
To make this work, a muscle is usually connected from one bone to another across a joint, allowing CONTRACTION to bring those two bones closer together. The peak of the muscle shape can occur in different locations based on the muscle.

Here is that arrow shape (that I mentioned earlier), overlapped to create … an arm. I know that it barely looks like an arm. This is the abstract simplification designed with FORCE shapes. Notice that the contracted side of the arm where the bicep would be is on the opposite of the FORCEFUL side on the left.

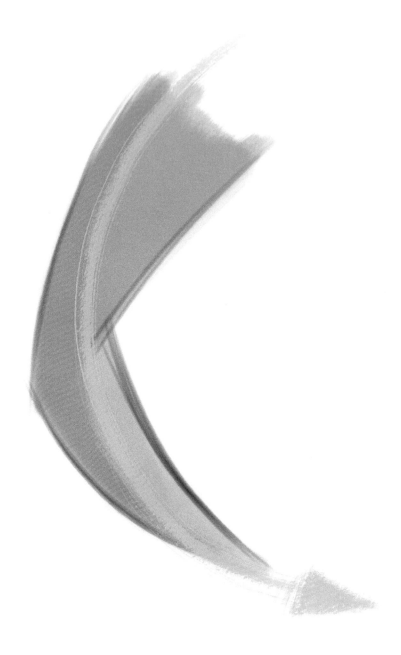

Further investigation shows how FORCE can drive through the entire arm, through the elbow joint, where the peak of Applied FORCE lies.

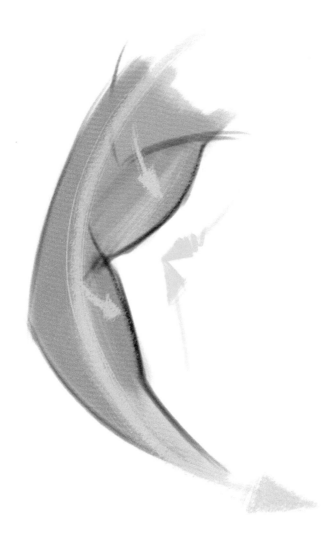

Now we add more shapes to the silhouette, the bicep, and the forearm flexor. This is the tricky part; the new shapes cannot defeat the larger curve of FORCE. The DON'TS must be dodged, or we lose the ability to drive FORCE through the entire limb. Notice that the contracted side of the arm where the bicep would be is on the opposite of the FORCEFUL side on the left. These FORCES create an asymmetrical silhouette for the arm.

We can take this same process to the trunk of the body.

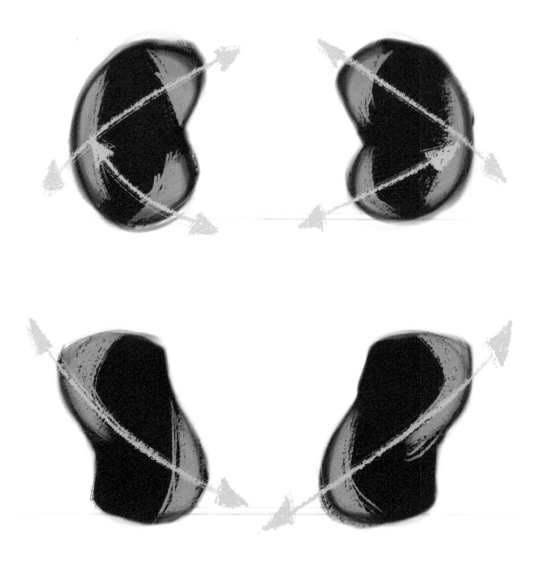

This bean shape has two versions. The top row has three Applied FORCE regions, those in orange. Those FORCES bounce left to right, across the torso, due to the bend between the rib cage and the pelvis. The bottom row shows a bean with two Applied FORCE regions. This occurs when the rib cage and the pelvis move in opposing directions, similar to that of a supermodel power walk.

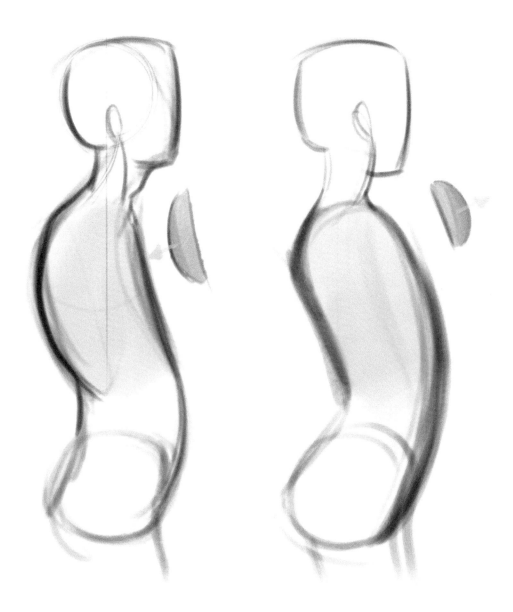

In the profile of the torso, you can see how the FORCE shape can clarify the function of the figure. For the pose on the left, FORCE is directed to the back, and on the right, the chest is pushed outward; thus, that is where FORCE is. The straight is then placed on the backside to support that outward thrust of Applied FORCE.

I will cover the FORCEFUL shapes in further detail throughout the rest of the book.

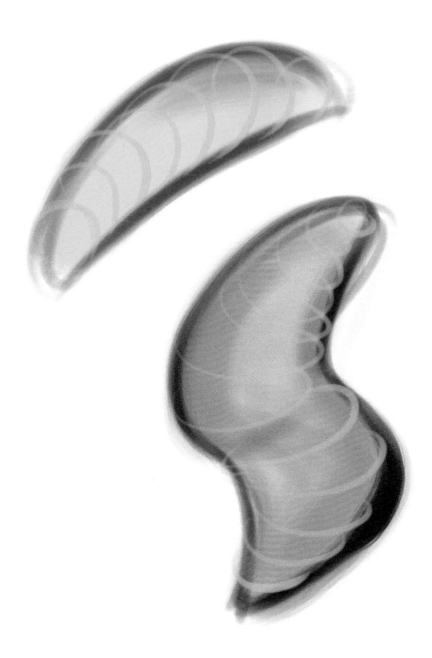

In the end, you want to fill the FORCE shapes with form. This form will become the anatomy of the figure.

EXERCISES AND TIPS

1. Learn the rules of shape.

2. Practice drawing FORCE shapes without breaking the rules.

3. Try to connect one FORCE shape to the next to create rhythm.

4. Fill the shape with volume.

5. Be aware of the edge of the shape with the most Applied FORCE.

Chapter 4

The Skeleton: Framework for the Figure

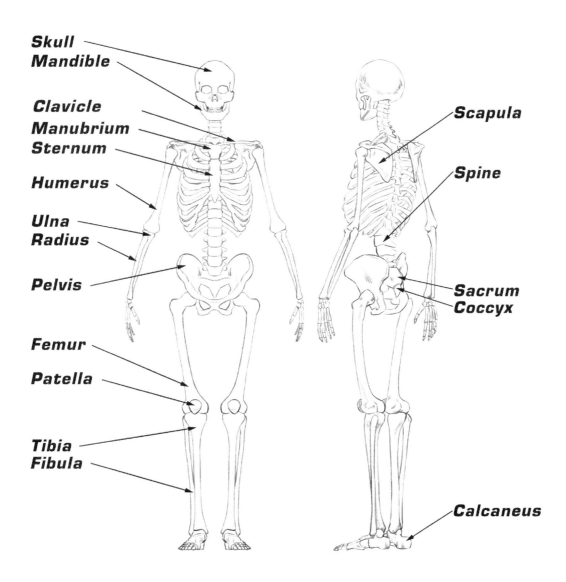

Skull
Mandible

Clavicle
Manubrium
Sternum

Humerus

Ulna
Radius

Pelvis

Femur

Patella

Tibia
Fibula

Scapula

Spine

Sacrum
Coccyx

Calcaneus

Since we are curious about how the human body functions, we need to know the underlying structures and how they function. In the case of the human body, that structure is the skeleton.

The skeleton provides a framework to attach all of the muscle groups to.

The skeleton is made of bones. There are different types of bones, but, I think, for our purposes of understanding FORCE pertaining to anatomy, let's stick with this simple concept.

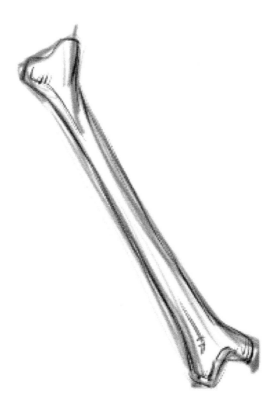

So, here is a human bone. These bones help create the rigidity of the body, like the wood or steel framework of a building. Without these bones, we could not function.

Our bones are not only fighting against the weight of our anatomy but also against resistance in the form of muscles, for instance, lifting a heavy weight. They also contend with twisting FORCES, torque.

JOINTS

Ellipsoid

Pivot

Saddle

Ball and socket

Hinge

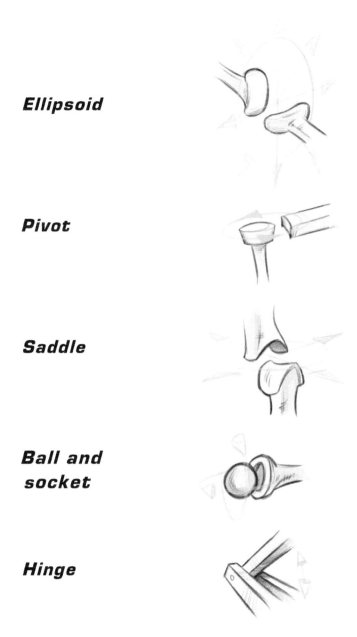

Once you have two bones that must connect and collaborate to define motion, you need a joint. Based on the type and range of motion needed for that joint, different joints have evolved. There are five of them, as illustrated above.

LIGAMENTS

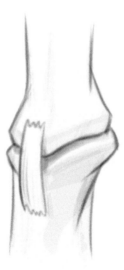

The ligaments bind or tape bones together and add strength to all of the joints. Think of them as "ligatape." It does not contract.

TENDONS

The blue areas above at the end of the muscles are the tendons. The tendon is a firm cord that connects the muscles to the bones, **ACROSS** joints. This is how muscles move bones. The typical term for the tendon/bone connection closer to the trunk of the body is the origin, and the further tendon/bone connection is the insertion. These two bones connected by a muscle across a joint are what cause our movements.

Does the human skeleton have FORCE? Everything has FORCE because of gravity, but what the skeleton rarely presents is rhythm. The major FORCES of the upper body are created through the design of the spine.

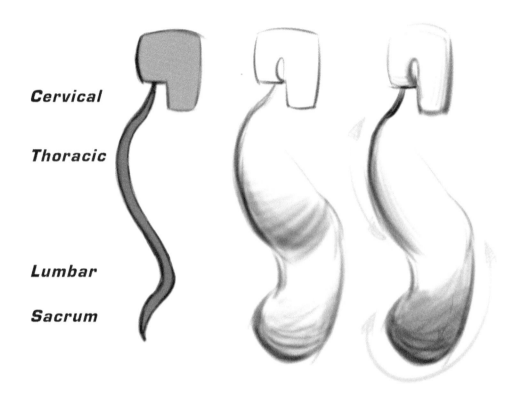

There are four areas of the spine that affect FORCE: (1) cervical, (2) thoracic, (3) lumbar, and (4) sacrum. Notice how each area occupies a curve found in the spine. In the profile view, you can clearly see the "S" path of the spine. This helps set up the major rhythms of the figure when muscular anatomy is put into place. Notice how the curve of the upper spine cradles the rib cage, and the pelvis hangs downward off the last arch of the spine.

The FORCE of the lumbar region of the spine or the lower back is projected **across** the figure to the abdomen. This important moment sets up the rhythms of the upper body in the profile view.

The spine allows for the bending and rotation that occur across those three rigid masses and has 26 levels of articulation.

HARD AND SOFT

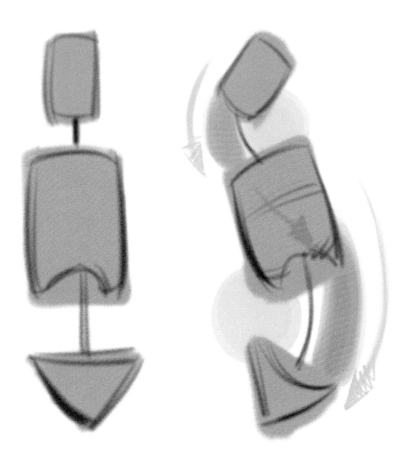

The three gray shapes above represent the rigid, hard forms of the body. Once muscles contract, presented by the green zones, the opposite sides of the figure stretches, shown with the orange APPLIED FORCE zones. Since the three rigid regions are attached to the spine, a subtle movement in one area creates a chain of events, or rhythms, affecting the other regions.

Be aware of the function of the three major regions of the skeleton:

1. The skull protects the brain.
2. The rib cage protects the heart and the lungs.
3. The "pelvis," Latin for "basin," holds the weight of the upper body and contains all of the internal organs.

To prove a point about the power of the curved FORCE line, look at this page in comparison to the next. I have drawn a stick-like figure to represent poses. See how stiff they feel in comparison to the same poses on the following page.

If we add FORCE to the skeleton, we could get some energy into the foundation. For me, the skeleton gives us proportions and angle changes. I don't typically teach artists to draw by creating this stick figure but instead draw the FORCES of the body, including anatomy, right from the start. This stick process can work when drawing from imagination to give you a foundation for the anatomy. Try to find the DIRECTIONAL FORCE CURVE from one joint to the next.

This is a one-minute drawing of a model, not from imagination, and you can see how FORCE is created using a line that creates shape and form. There is no stick figure, but instead there are immediate reactions to the actual figure.

EXERCISES AND TIPS

1. Draw numerous poses using the FORCE stick figure when drawing from imagination. Keep in mind the power of curved lines; beware of the straight when drawing bones.

2. Draw and investigate the different joints in the body and where they are found. This gives you a profound understanding of motion range per joint. Keep in mind that the muscles move across the joints.

Chapter 5
How This Book Functions

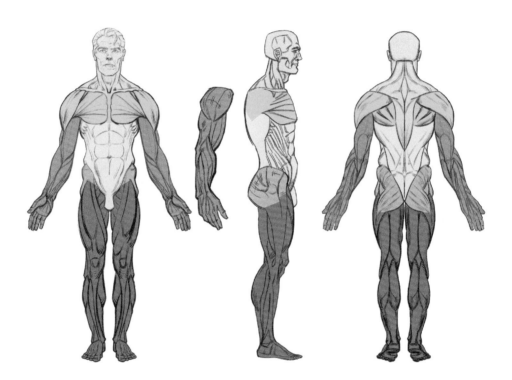

I have color-coded regions of the figure. Moving through the chapters, we will start at the top of the figure: the head, the neck, and the shoulders. Each region will define a new chapter, and within each chapter, there will be three sections, one per different view of the body, the front, side, and rear views. Each chapter discusses the FORCE, anatomy, and functional shapes of those muscles. I have also placed the color of the specific region on the edge of the pages for ease of use so you can efficiently find regions and views of the body you want to learn about.

Here are some anatomical landmarks to remember when drawing the figure.

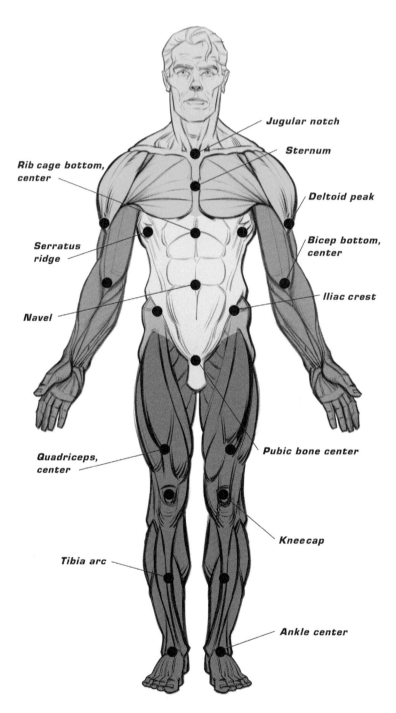

Jugular notch

Sternum

Rib cage bottom, center

Deltoid peak

Serratus ridge

Bicep bottom, center

Iliac crest

Navel

Quadriceps, center

Pubic bone center

Kneecap

Tibia arc

Ankle center

Notice that most of these landmarks are what I call "natural centers." They help me orient the figure in space. Let's look at the other two views.

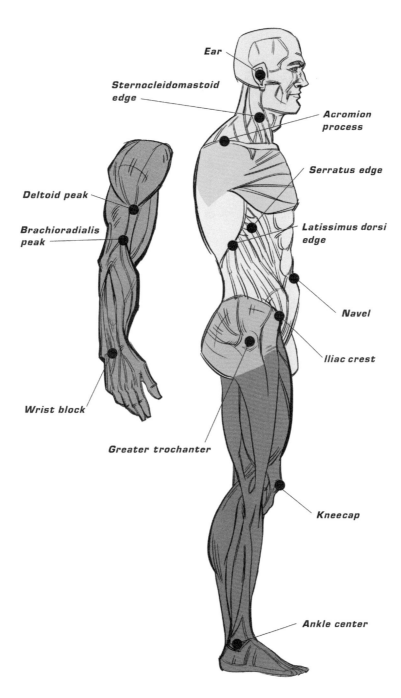

Ear

Sternocleidomastoid edge

Acromion process

Deltoid peak

Serratus edge

Brachioradialis peak

Latissimus dorsi edge

Navel

Iliac crest

Wrist block

Greater trochanter

Kneecap

Ankle center

In the side view, there are not many centers but, instead, the edges of muscles that I use to show form, especially during torso rotation. Due to the shallow depth, FORCE surface lines can become valuable in this view of the figure.

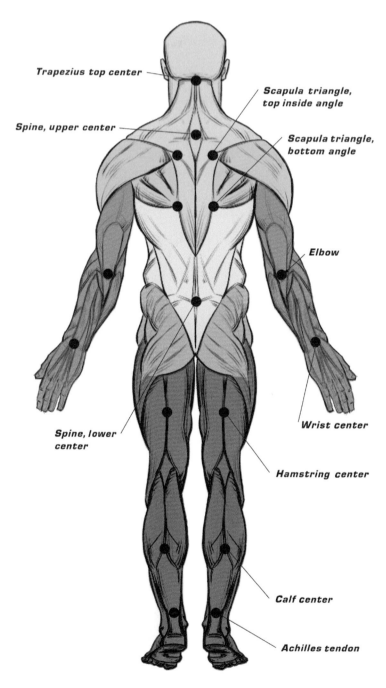

Trapezius top center

Scapula triangle, top inside angle

Spine, upper center

Scapula triangle, bottom angle

Elbow

Wrist center

Spine, lower center

Hamstring center

Calf center

Achilles tendon

In the back view, you can see the return of natural centers. The legs in this view are quite simple to illustrate due to the centered orientation of the anatomy. The most complex region of anatomy is the upper back, and I will utilize many pages and drawings in an attempt to simplify it.

You'll notice that I have not and will not discuss proportions, especially in terms of how many heads tall the figure is or some other measuring system. The reason for my purposeful exclusion of these concepts is that every person is proportionately unique, and, by defining specific proportions to you, I fear you falling into the trap of creating figures of the same proportions. Instead, learn to see clearly, and be surprised by the proportions you find in each individual.

This allows you to also push proportions when designing character from imagination.

For each chapter of
the book, I will write a
blurb about my top-level
thoughts pertaining to
that region of the
figure. In this first
region, the front of
the head, neck, and
upper back, I will share
with you tricks to keep
FORCE flowing through
this very structural and
symmetrical area of the
body. The neck is what
connects the head
to the body and
is the flexible
moment to work
with in order to create
rhythm. We will also
look at the front view of
the face. The face is full
of numerous muscles to
express our emotions.
You will learn about my
approach to breaking
up the face into shapes
that allow you to
push expression in a
FORCEFUL approach.

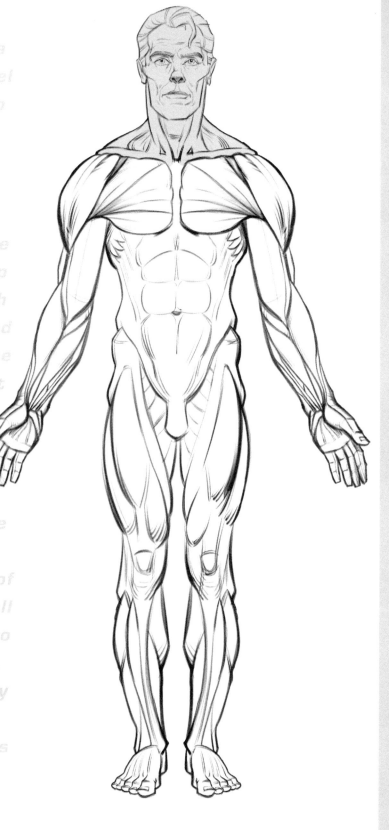

Occipitofrontalis
Pulls scalp upward, raises all skin over the brows

Procerus
Pulls down eyebrows

Depressor Supercilii
Lowers eyebrows

Orbicularis Oculi
Closes eyelid

Levator Labii Superioris
Raises and moves upper lip forward

Zygomaticus Major
Pulls upper lip upward and sideways

Zygomaticus Minor
Pulls upper lip upward, outward and sideways

Risorius
Pulls mouth open laterally

Depressor Anguli Oris
Draws angle of mouth downward and laterally

Mentalis
Raises and protrudes lower lip

Trapezius
Levitate Clavicle, extends neck and stabilizes shoulder

Depressor Labii Inferioris
Pulls lower lip to center axis

Sternocleidomastoid
Pulls head downward toward shoulders and rotates head

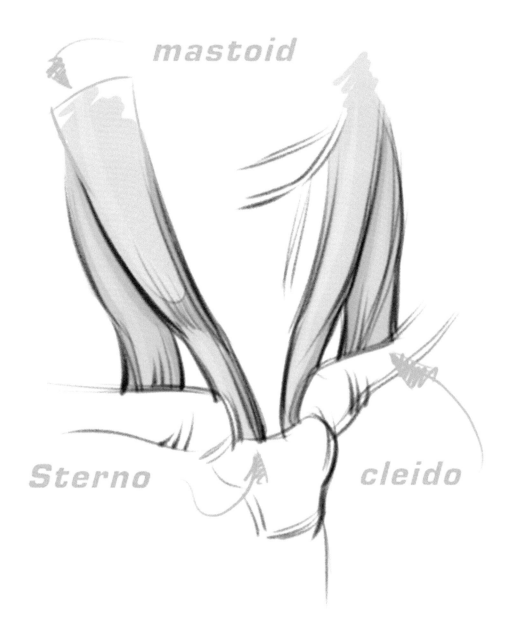

mastoid

Sterno

cleido

The name "sternocleidomastoid" comes from the bone names the muscles are connected to, as shown above. Notice the small triangles created between the two lower connections. I use this triangle often to quickly illustrate the anatomy found here.

The sternocleidomastoid muscles assist in the bending and rotation of the neck and the head. They keep the chin up and assist in the ease of breathing.

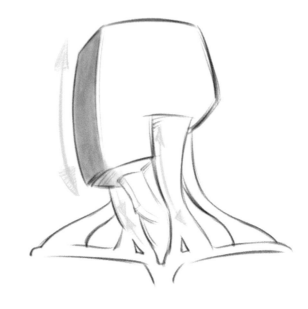

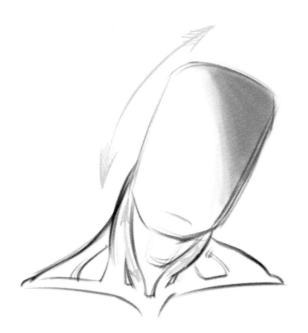

The sternocleidomastoid muscles support all of the major movements of the head. This includes rotation and tilting. I tinted the APPLIED FORCES orange, and you can see how this region can move from the side of the head to the face.

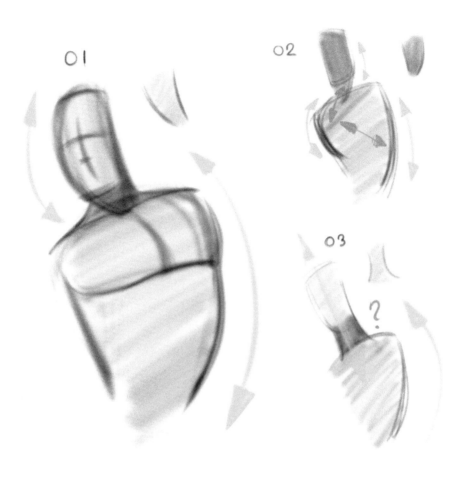

From the front view, you can **see** how the natural rhythms of the neck function in between the rib cage and the head. It **is easy** to fall into the trap of symmetry though. The drawings above show the following:

1. Here, we can see how FORCE moves from the one side of the figure to the opposite side of the neck.

2. It could look like it bunny-hops from the rib cage to the neck, but the middle DIRECTIONAL FORCE of the upper back along the top edge of the body creates the connection.

3. Notice the trap. Be careful to **not** create the symmetrical double-concave shape. As you can see, the FORCEFUL connection or rhythm is lost here between the head and the rib cage.

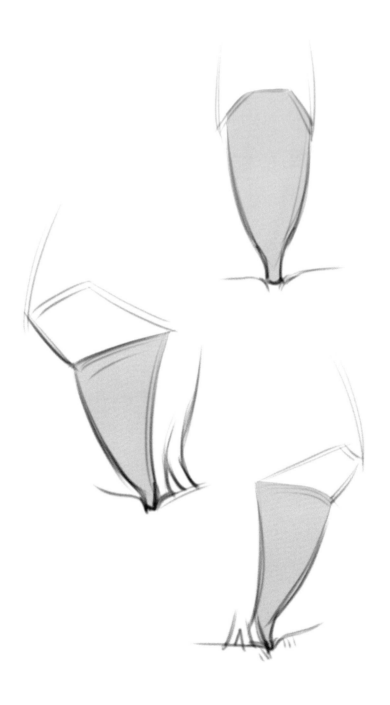

As we know from Chapter 3, we want to stay away from symmetrical shapes, yet, innately, the shape created between the two sterno muscles, the area of the throat, creates a symmetrical triangle, as seen in the top drawing. I try to see any slight angle change so that the neck is NOT directly facing me or has any subtle rotation within it. The middle and bottom drawings show how to see the FORCE triangle that the sternos can create with some rotation away from your view.

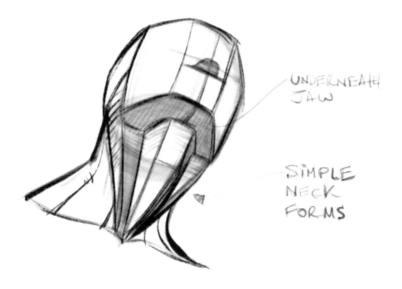

UNDERNEATH
JAW

SIMPLE
NECK
FORMS

Here is a drawing that shows the simple forms of the jaw and how it connects to the neck. Always keep in mind the lower plane of the jaw.

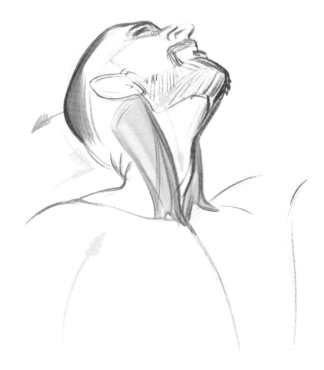

Directional FORCE shoots up over the upper back into the neck, and then the sternocleidomastoid muscles. Once there, FORCE applies itself through the face and to the top of the head.

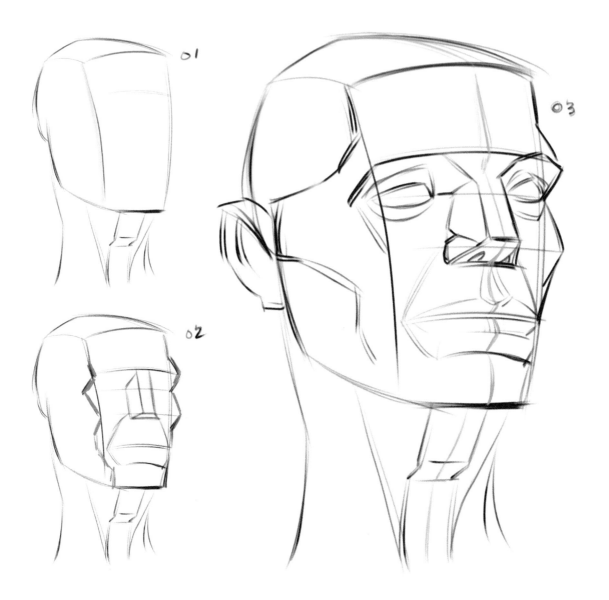

The human head presents the importance of knowing perspective. In drawing 01, you can see the cube as an inspiration for the first formation of the head. The teal line is the turning edge of the cube.

Drawing 02 shows the understanding that one edge of the front plane must match the other since they describe the same surface.

Drawing 03 presents a more faceted face. The green line presents the centerline of the face helping me build the forms with structural integrity. You can purchase planar heads to assist you with seeing perspective and understanding the complexities of the head through more simple forms. This is a skill that is used for drawing anything, from the human body to vehicles and buildings.

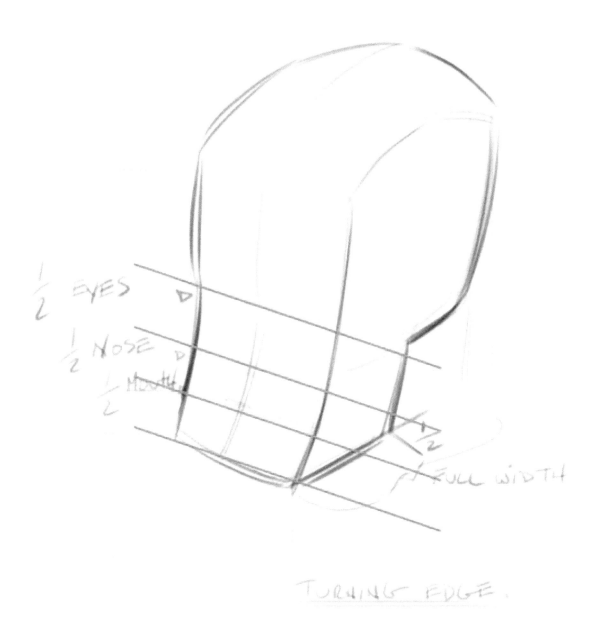

½ EYES ▷

½ NOSE ▷

½ Mouth

½ FULL WIDTH

TURNING EDGE.

Here is another example showing how the perspective controls the parallel moments across facial features. These angles are crucial for drawing believable faces. The lines can slowly converge on the back end to exaggerate perspective.

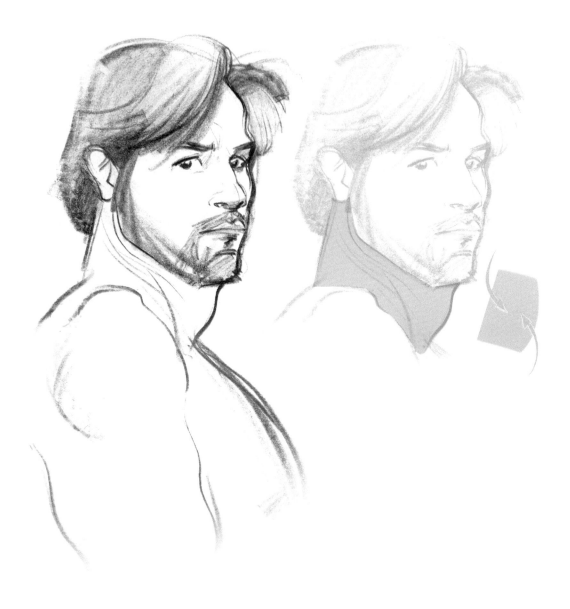

Look at the angles created between the eyes, the nostrils, and the mouth line. See how these moments relative to one another are parallel. To the right side, I called out the shape of the neck. It boils down to a straight-to-curve shape with a few wrinkles across the neck that show how rhythm moves across the neck form.

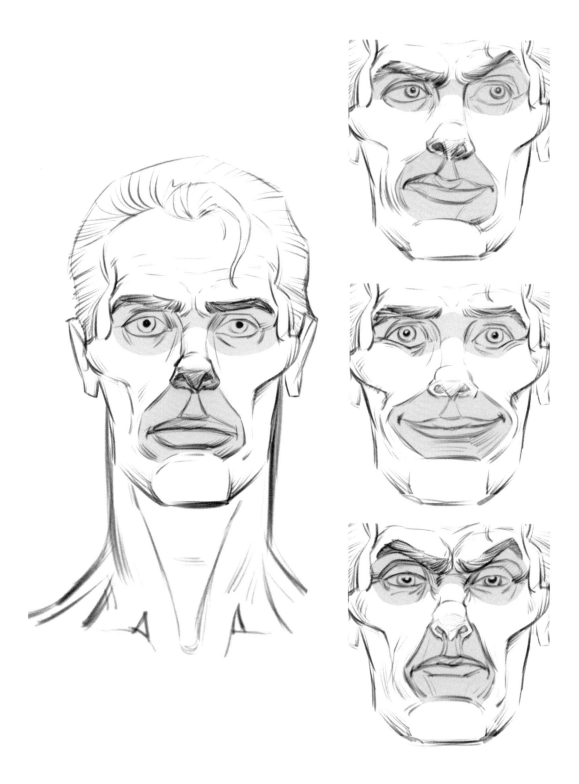

I have simplified the complex function of all the facial muscles into an eye mask and a mouth mask. Seeing the complexities of the face in such simplicity will allow you to observe and draw any facial expressions quickly. You could draw the face starting with these shapes and then fill in the actual anatomy.

This image shows different FORCES in the face. Notice the rhythms in the eyebrows and the opposing FORCES in the mouth shape.

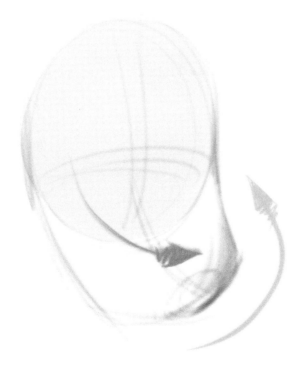

Keep in mind that the top of the skull and the jaw are held together by muscles, and therefore FORCE can be presented through Directional motion. Above, we can see the jaw being swept to the right side of the page.

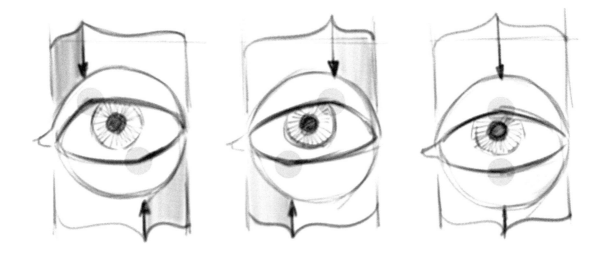

When drawing the eyes, be aware of the sphere and how the lids wrap around them. Also, pay close attention to the asymmetry in the peaks of the lid edges. The drawings above show the lid apexes, in the blue circles, in different positions relative to one another. These subtle contrasts convey a more organic feel to the face. The drawing on the far right shows the lids aligned horizontally. This is a static design.

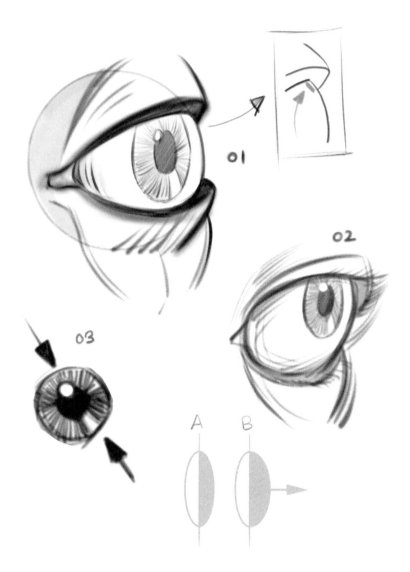

Drawing 01 shows the roundness of the eyeball and the offset of lines that occurs around the edge of a form to present dimensionality, here shown with the orange line.

Drawing 02 focuses on the eyelids and the lashes. They protrude out of the edge of the eyelid. Be aware of the thickness of the eyelid between the lash and the eyeball.

Drawing 03 shows the highlight on the pupil of the eye and how light shines through the eye out to the opposite side. Pay attention to the angle of the light.

Lastly, drawing A presents a symmetrical ellipse where both sides of the ellipse are the same.

Drawing B is actually more accurate where one side is wider than the other. Aside from this asymmetrical ellipse being more accurate, it follows the rules of good shape since one side of the ellipse is more curved than the other. Doing this also makes the pupil point in a clearer direction, in this case, to the right of the page.

TRIANGLE

The nose is a complex structure on top of the complex structure of the face. As usual, the way to approach drawing it is through hierarchical simplicity.

Left drawing: Shows the four main planes of the nose.

Center drawing: After visualizing the four planes, we then define the front structure of the nose.

Right drawing: I use a triangle shape to define the front-surface turning edge of the nose and the center of the bottom surface where it meets the face.

The main idea to remember when drawing the mouth is that it wraps around the curvature of the teeth. In the drawings above, you can see the use of the centerline and how that divides the lips into quadrants and helps define the top and bottom surfaces.

EXERCISES AND TIPS

1. Using a simple cube, cardboard, or a wooden, draw a grid on it, similar to the one drawn in Chapter 2. Find a perspective that you like, and try to draw the angles on the cube to define the location of facial features. Keep the eye, nostril, and mouth lines parallel to one another.

2. Using a mirror, practice drawing your face.

3. Try drawing facial expressions using eye and mouth masks.

4. Keep in mind that the skull is rigid. Also, think about the jaw containing some flexibility.

5. Look for variety in facial features.

In this view, we can see the cantilever function of the upper back relative to the weight of the head. The primary muscles of the neck, the sternocleidomastoid muscles, are used to create rhythm through the neck, connecting the head and the torso.

All of this muscular anatomy attaches to the spine, the clavicles, and the scapulae. The neck region allows for enormous flexibility, allowing us to face many directions and emote through how we hold our head.

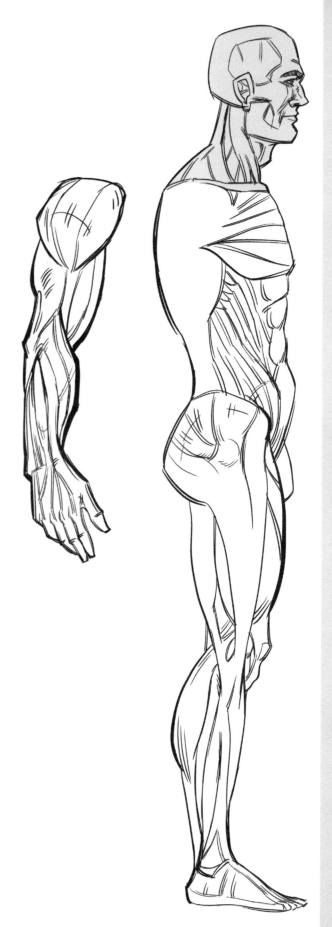

Occipitofrontalis
Pulls scalp upward, raises all skin over the brows

Temporalis
Elevates and retracts mandible

Orbicularis Oculi
Closes eyelid

Masseter
Raises the lower jaw

Levator Labii Superioris
Raises and moves upper lip forward

Zygomaticus Major
Pulls upper lip upward and sideways

Risorius
Pulls mouth open laterally

Depressor Anguli Oris
Draws angle of mouth downward and laterally

Trapezius
Levitates clavicle, extends neck, and stabilizes shoulder

Sternocleidomastoid
Pulls head downward towards shoulders, and rotates head

Here is a simplified version of the profile view showing FORCES for the head, the neck, and the back. See how the FORCE from the back moves through the neck and projects its way out through the face.

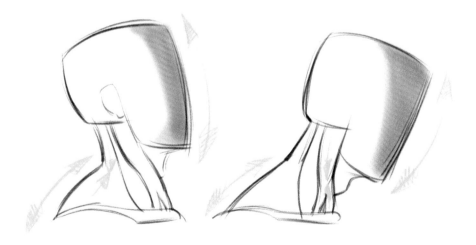

These two drawings show the rhythm from the upper back to the face, where FORCE is last applied. Green presents CONTRACTIONS.

The FORCE of the upper back connects with the sterno. See the positive and negative shapes. They all follow the rules of FORCE. The sterno clearly presents the Directional FORCE found in its front edge.

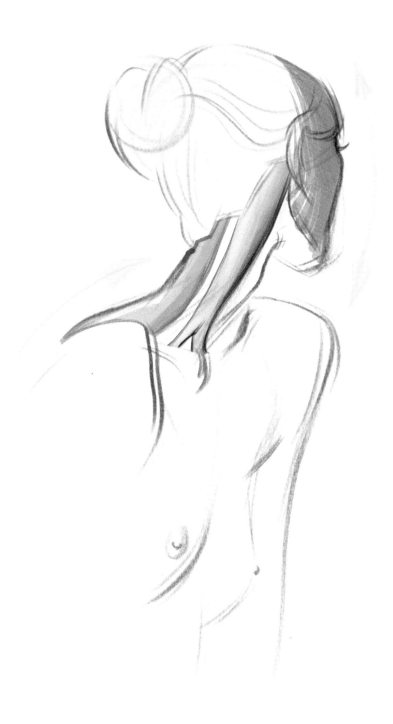

The sterno on the near side is stretching, and the one on the far side of the neck is contracting, thus rotating the head away from us. Also, here you can see how the Directional FORCE from the back connects to the head and applies itself to the front of the face.

In this side view, we can see the overlap of the sterno muscle and the trapezius. The closer sterno is contracting, rotating the head toward us. Let's move on to the face in profile.

The orange lines in diagram 01 show you how I use FORCE lines to define the contour of the face. The flipping of convex and concave curves presented in example line 02 creates a beautiful, rhythmic, and structural edge. A typical mistake I see made by artists when drawing contours is the smoothing out of these flipped moments. The edges of the structures are the moments where the line changes from one direction to another.

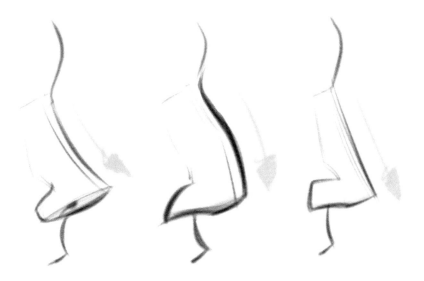

When drawing the side view, the nose and its FORCE play a major role in the face's character. Above, we see a convex, concave, and straight line of FORCE quickly creating different characters.

01 02

7 MIN

Diagram 01 shows a softer contour line, and you can see that it is hard to define the structural edges.

In diagram 02, I sharpened the edges and made the convex and concave curves more obvious, thus defining a clearer structure that I can follow into the drawing of the face more easily. No matter how soft or hard the corners of an object are in reality, in my mind, I think about the crisp edges and then sand them as though they were made of wood, and I used a sandpaper to define their specific radius.

The idea that I went after in this pose was the upward push of the arm and the hand into the face and how the face reacted.

This profile of David, a great model in Los Angeles, shows the clear structure of his brow, nose, and jaw because of the parallel lines that can be found among them. This can be seen with the orange lines overlaying the drawing in the top-right corner. They help me set up the perspective that the head resides in. The blue line shows the turning edge, and green is the center.

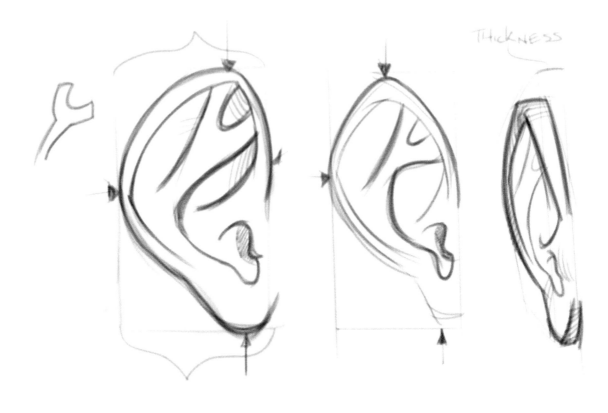

I can't discuss the side of the head without some focus on the ears. Ears present a great opportunity for uniqueness. They come in different kinds of shapes and sizes. Let me discuss with you what the drawings above present.

Left drawing: We have a drawing that appears to be a red "Y." This shape can be seen in the next two drawings. I look for this shape in ears. It is a fast way of describing what seems like odd, abstract structures.

Center drawing: The flat ear drawings are illustrated within a rectangular box. This box also lets me see the specific proportion of each model's ear. The arrows show where the peaks of the model's ear touch the perimeter of the rectangle. Notice the FORCE shapes found within the edges of the ear: wide-to-narrow shapes with an arc.

Right drawing: We have a drawing that shows an ear in perspective. The keynote I have to share with you here is that the ear has thickness. Yes, keep in mind its narrow width.

EXERCISES AND TIPS

1. Keep in mind the birdlike connection between the upper back and the neck.

2. Practice using concave and convex curves to clarify structure. This is most clearly found in the face but can be used in all areas of the body.

3. Remember that FORCE moves from the upper back to the front edge of the sternocleidomastoid muscle and then up into the face and the skull.

In the back view of the
head, the neck, and
the upper back, we see
the famous diamond/
dagger shape of the
trapezius muscles and how
they bridge the gap from
the skull to the shoulder
blades, to the spine.
Understanding the traps
connection to these
areas and how they
function is important
to drawing the
back. These flat
muscles are
strong visual
markers for defining
the rest of the
complex muscular
system of the back.

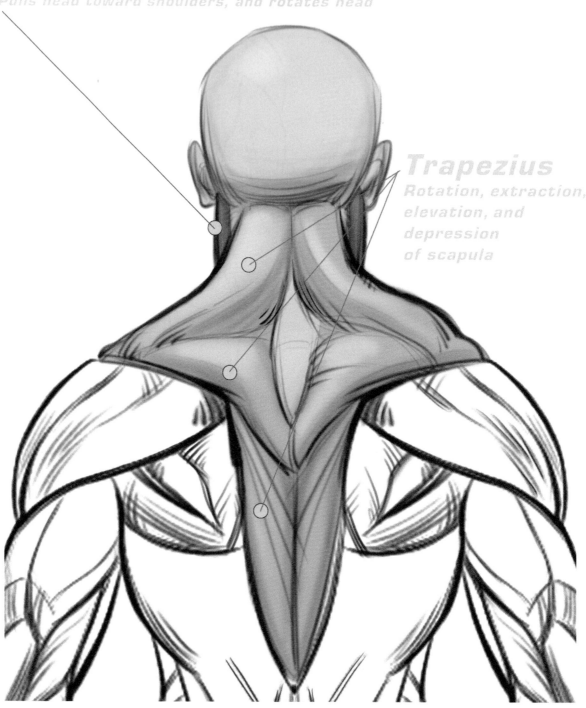

Sternocleidomastoid
Pulls head toward shoulders, and rotates head

Trapezius
Rotation, extraction, elevation, and depression of scapula

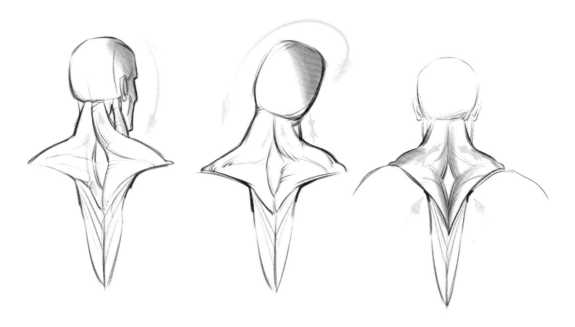

You can see how the trapezius muscles function in the above images. The traps help rotate the head, tilt it, and shrug the shoulders upward. They are also attached to the scapulae along the top ridge, moving them in numerous directions. The diamond shape compresses and stretches based on how it functions.

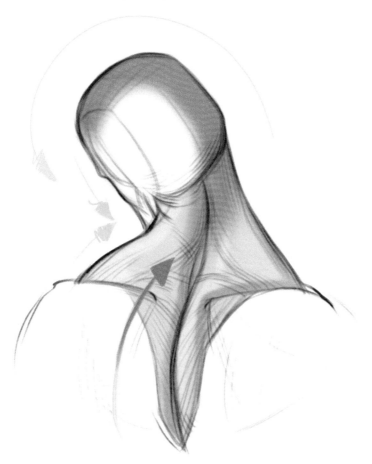

Here, you can see how the FORCE of the back drives into the head through the neck by contracting the muscles on the left side of the neck.

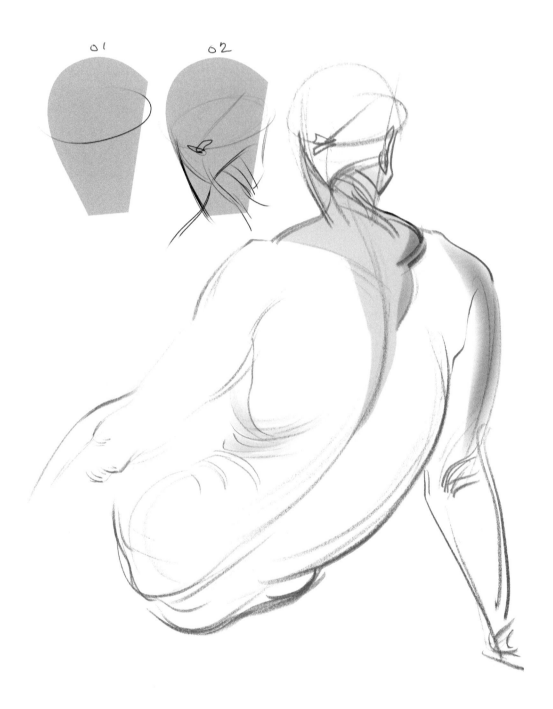

Orange areas here show the function of this pose, the lean into the right shoulder with the head turning over it. The gray shapes to the left show you how I perceived the model's head. If you look at the drawing, you can see the vertical line on the right side that I used as the foundation for the straight-to-curve shape.

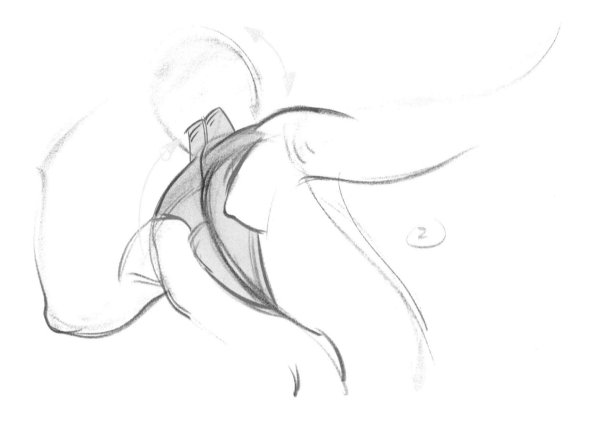

The diamond shape of the trapezius muscle lays across the back of the neck and the center of the upper back. See how FORCE travels rhythmically from the back, through the neck and into the head. The negative shape of the scapulae on either side of the traps helps create the shape of the traps.

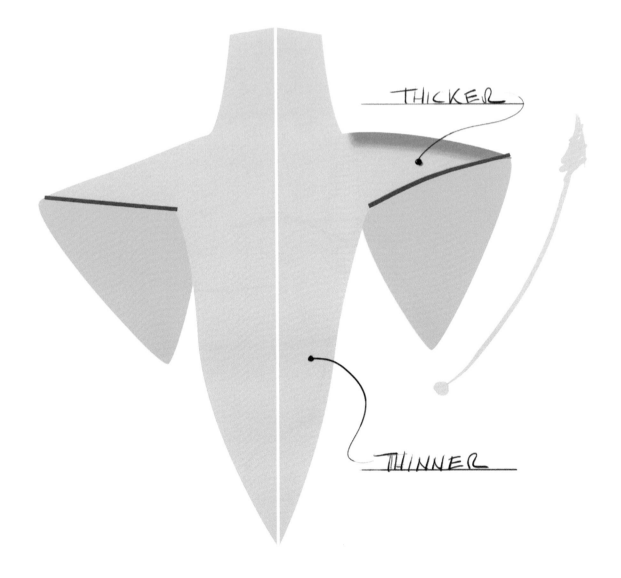

The relationship between the trapezius and the scapula is a crucial one to understanding the back. The above simplification presents how the raising of the arm affects the upward rotation of the scapula, shown on the right, and how the trapezius contracts at the top where it becomes thicker and stretches at the bottom where it becomes thinner.

The traps attach to a ridge near the top of the scapula called the SCAPULA SPINE, presented by the red lines, defining the connective relationship between the two areas of the back.

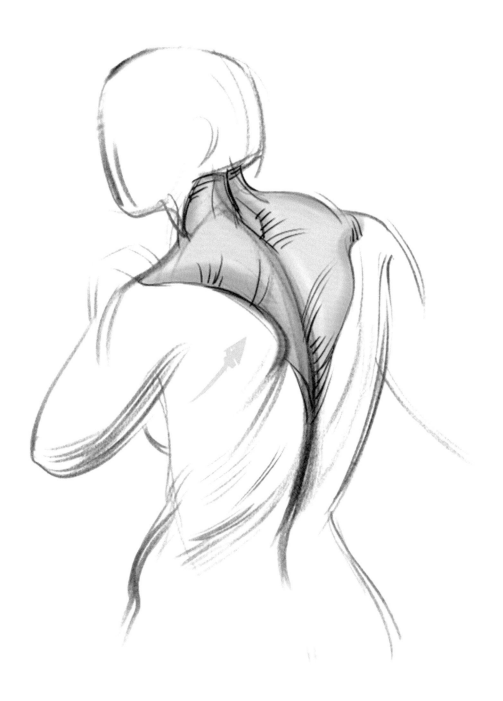

Once more, see how the scapula helps define the shape of the traps. The left arm, which is more raised, pushes in the shape of the trap.

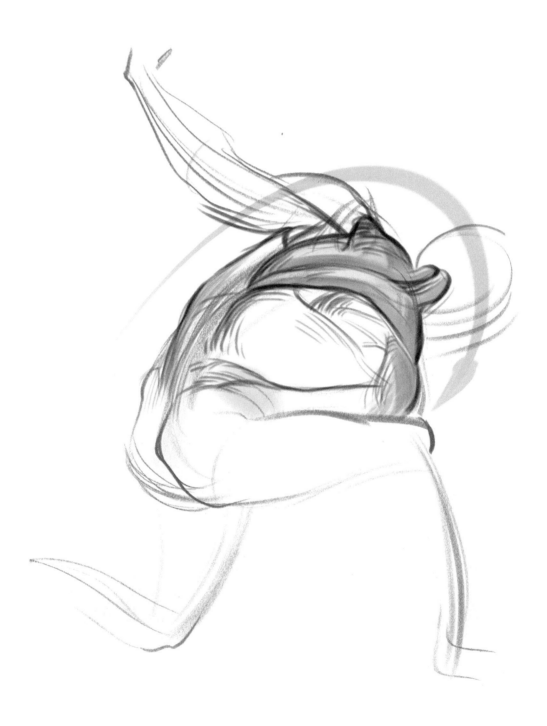

See how the trapezius slides over the roundness of the back and defines the location of the scapulae. You can also see the CONTRACTION of the right-side obliques and the Applied FORCES in the left side of the body that then drive into the right shoulder.

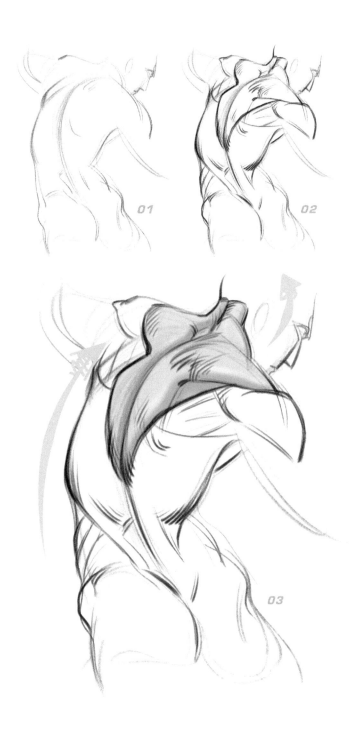

In this step-by-step drawing, you can see the original figure drawing, 01, the line art of the anatomy, 02, and then the painted trapezius in 03. Directional FORCE sweeps up the left side of the body into the upper back, the neck, and then into the head.

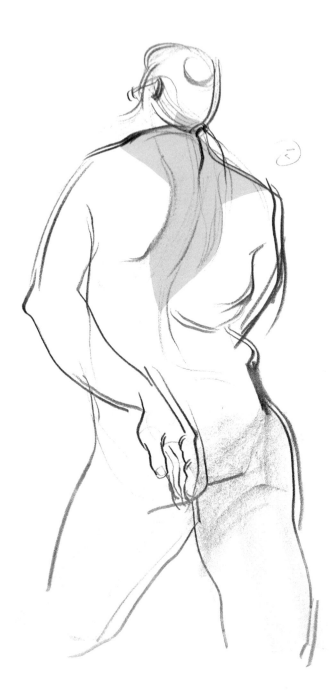

This drawing contains a flat color overlay without the anatomy line pass. You can see that the left scapula and the spine are enough to present the musculature of this model's back. On heavier models, where muscular definition is not as obvious, you must truly know your anatomy to understand how to present it with as little detail as possible.

EXERCISES AND TIPS

1. Try finding the diamond shape of the traps, and lay it down on the surface of the back.

2. Use the traps to help locate the scapulae spines and the angles they create.

3. Pay attention to the function of the traps and how they stretch and compress to show their function.

There is great range
of motion in the
shoulders allowing for
freedom in the arms.
The chest, consisting
primarily of the pectoral
muscles, contract allowing
for the arms to come
together in the front
of the body. The act of
clapping or doing push-ups
also brings arms closer
together in front of
the chest while
pushing against
the weight
of your body.
The shoulder or
the deltoid is where the
complex range of motion
begins for the arm. As we
rotate around the figure,
we'll gain more awareness
of the muscles that
contribute to this amazing
area of the human body.

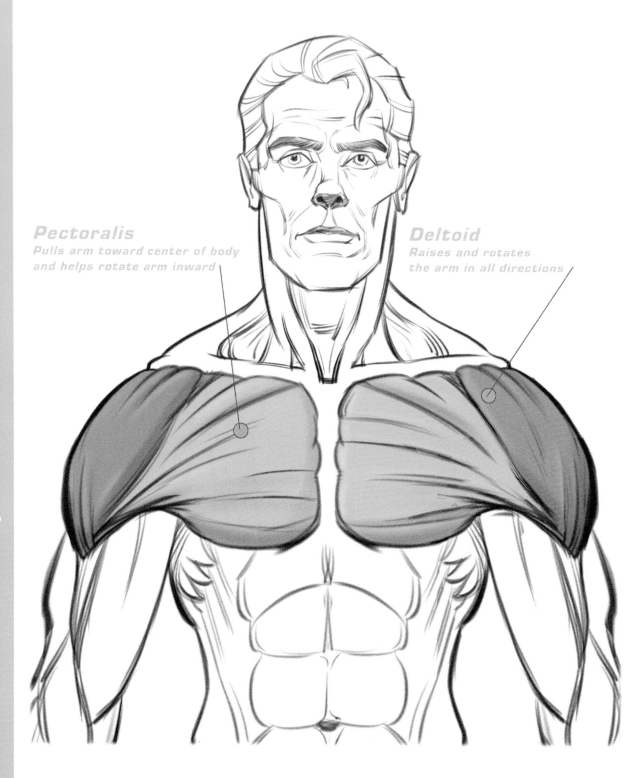

Pectoralis
*Pulls arm toward center of body
and helps rotate arm inward*

Deltoid
*Raises and rotates
the arm in all directions*

UPPER GIRDLE

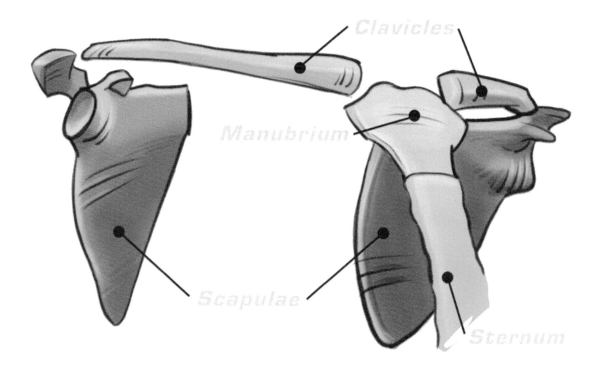

Clavicles

Manubrium

Scapulae

Sternum

Here is what is commonly called the upper girdle. Notice the "T"-shaped structure created by the sternum, the manubrium and the clavicles. The scapula "wings" on the back connected to the "T" structure allow for a wide range of motion in our arms.

If you have the *FORCE: Animal Drawing* (2011) book, you'll know that, in four-legged mammals, there is NO skeletal connection between the front limbs and the rib cage, causing their high level of flexibility. In humans, the only place where the bones connect to a rigid structure is where the clavicle connects to the manubrium through a saddle joint. Then, there are a ton of "ligatapes," where the clavicle and the scapula connect. The humerus bone of the upper arm sits in the ball-and-socket joint of the scapula. The scapulae, in turn, slide around the back of the rib cage, defined by the movements of all the prior joints.

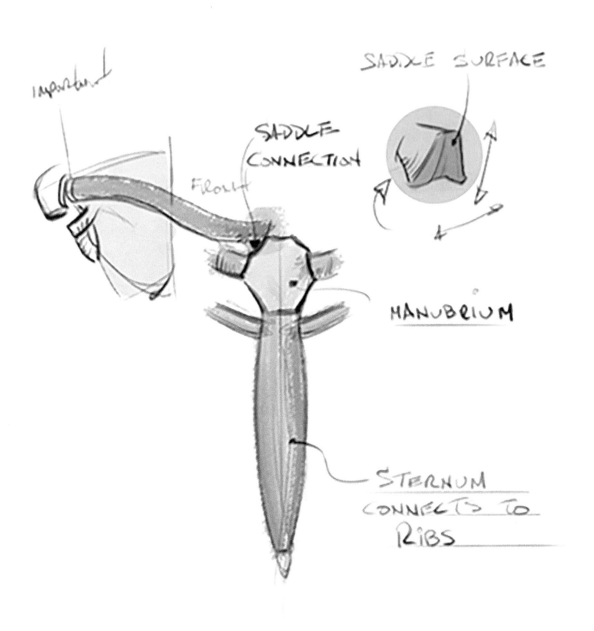

SADDLE SURFACE

important

SADDLE CONNECTION

FRONT

MANUBRIUM

STERNUM CONNECTS TO RIBS

Here is a front view of the shoulder girdle. Notice the saddle joint (blue zone) that connects the manubrium and the clavicles, in orange. A deep understanding of the shoulder girdle and how it connects to the rib cage is essential for understanding all of the muscular anatomy of the upper body. It is important to remember that the clavicle connects to the scapula to build the structure of the shoulder girdle.

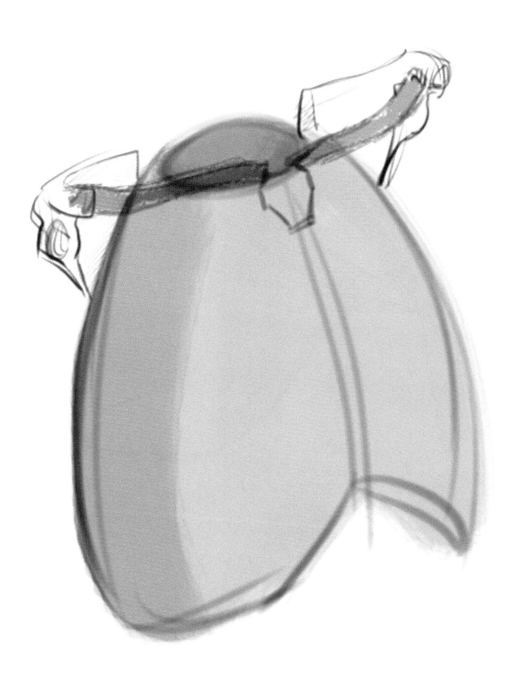

Here is a simple drawing presenting how the upper girdle sits on top of and around the rib cage. The clavicles are colored orange.

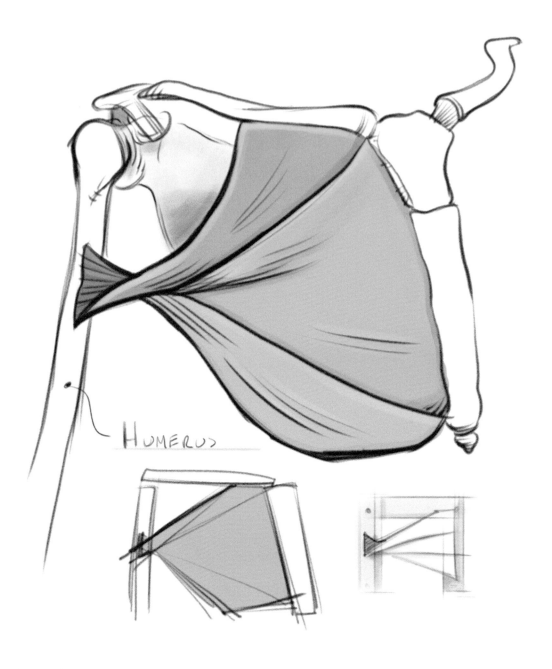

HUMERUS

Earlier in Chapter 4, we discussed the shoulder girdle. The main point to understand is how the clavicles attach to the manubrium and the sternum. From there, they swing out to the shoulders where the clavicles connect to the scapulae. Scapulae contain the construct of the shoulder joint, where the humerus resides. Above, we can see how the sternum, the manubrium, the clavicle, the humerus, and the ribs create a frame that the pectorals reside within, as seen in the lower drawing. The origin of the pectorals lies in the bones of the upper girdle, and the insertion point is on the humerus bone.

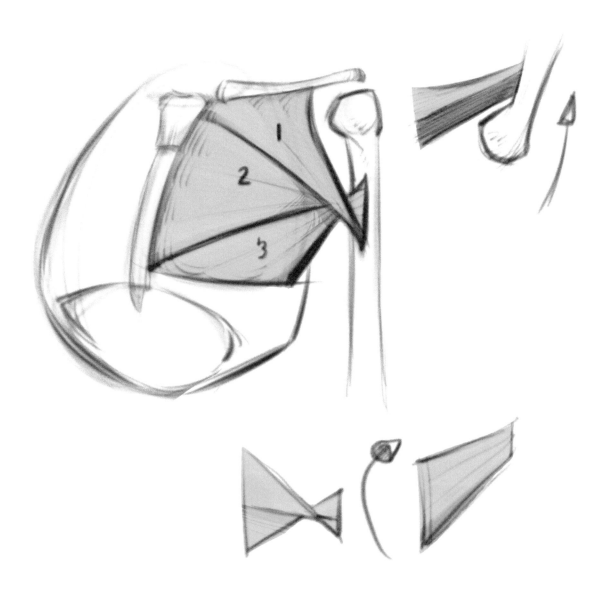

When the arms are down, the pec muscles actually overlap one another as they make their way over to the bone of the upper arm, the humerus. When the arm is raised, the muscles are parallel to one another, as seen in the bottom-right drawing. I also like to think of the pecs in three sections, as you can see numbered above. There is basically a top, middle, and bottom section.

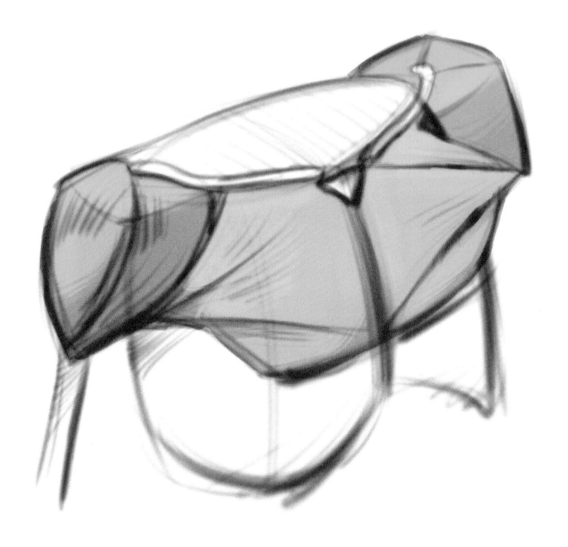

We finally get to muscle grouping and you can see how it is reminiscent to football pads. I take any opportunity that I can to group muscles. This allows me more broad, functional thinking. Notice how they fit perfectly next to one another. There is a small triangle of empty space where they meet at the clavicle. The pectorals also connect above the deltoids' insertion points on the humerus. The deltoid protects the entire shoulder joint and gives it function.

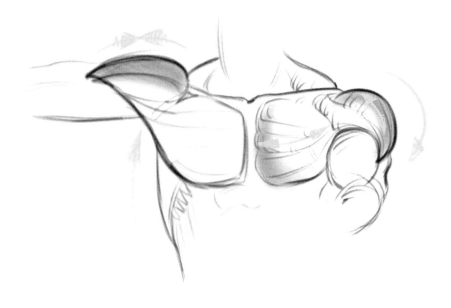

See how the different DIRECTIONAL and APPLIED FORCES function across the chest and into the shoulders. The shoulder on the left side of the page contracts, thus lifting the arm. The pectorals on the right side contract along with the front of the deltoid to bring that arm forward, toward us.

Here is a top–down drawing to more clearly show how the CONTRACTION of the pectoralis muscle brings the arm forward. This is why push-ups and/or butterflies are great exercises for this muscle.

This figure drawing presents the football pads concept and the overlap found in the pectorals. Also, notice how the pectorals are divided into the three sections: the top, middle, and bottom section. You can clearly see here where the pectorals end, entwined, under the tip of deltoid. On a side note, notice the attention that I gave to the volume of the leg. See how the surface lines support the idea of the leg moving toward us.

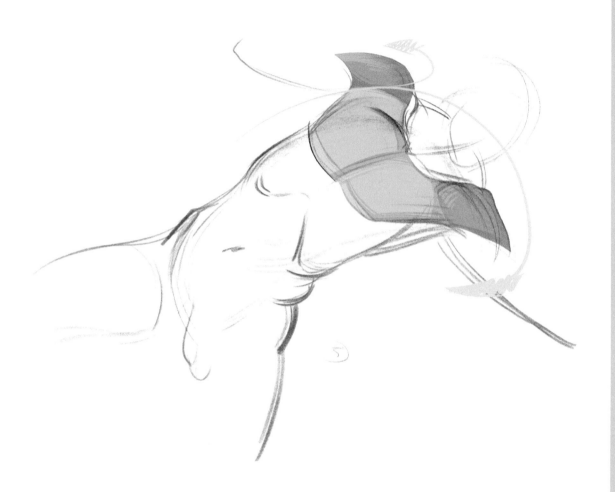

Here is one more drawing to clarify the football pads analogy. FORCE drives over the top of the rib cage, out the top arm, and primarily down into the lower arm.

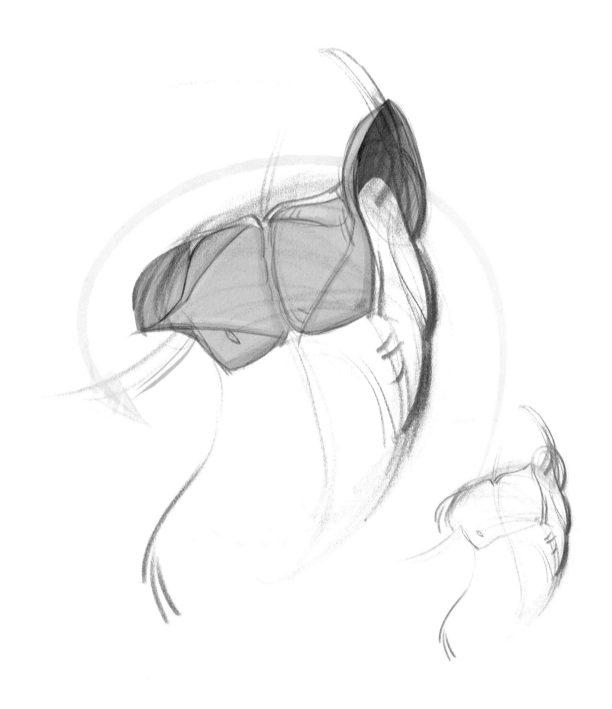

When the arms are raised, the pads are lifted, exposing the armpit and stretching the pectorals, the latissimus dorsi, and the trapezius. I think about this "draping"-like quality of the deltoids on the top of the arm and draw through the arm to understand this full moment. Once more you can see the three sections of the pectorals. The original drawing without overlay is in the bottom right.

EXERCISES AND TIPS

1. Think about grouping the pecs and the deltoids in their football gear-like structure to find their FORCEFUL relationships.

2. Try dividing the pecs into three regions to see how they are connected to the bone frame.

3. Notice how the deltoids function relative to the direction that the arm is raised.

4. Use the clavicles, the sternum axis, and the bottom of the pecs to define the perspective of the rib cage.

In the side view of the deltoid, we can see its inverted-teardrop shape comprised of the pointed bottom that connects to the humerus bone. The deltoid allows for the forward and backward raising of the arm because it is built of the front, back, and side heads.

The clavicles or the collarbones connect to the scapulae and the humerus here, and the deltoid helps strengthen that connection. The body structurally turns the corner from the front to the side view of the figure.

This shoulder joint, the glenohumeral joint, is crucial to the arm's flexibility.

I use the side view of the shoulder as a primary location of **FORCE** coming from the back, hitting the shoulder, and driving down into the arm. Lastly, the pectorals connect under the tip of the deltoid, tightly wound when the arm is in its rested, lowered position.

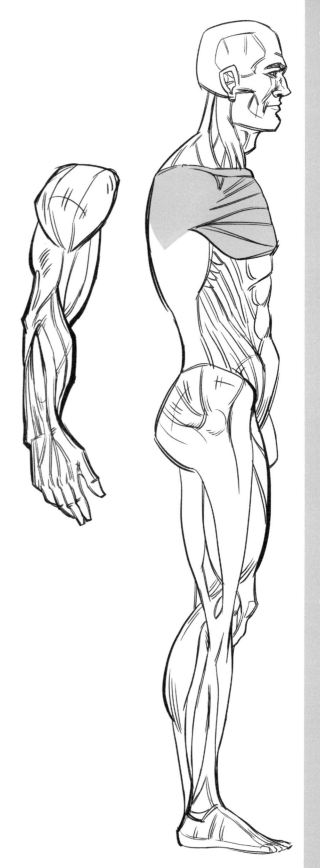

Deltoid Front
Raises arm to the front

Deltoid Center
Raises arm to the side

Deltoid Rear
Raises arm to the rear

Pectoralis
Pulls arm toward center
of body and helps
rotate arm inward

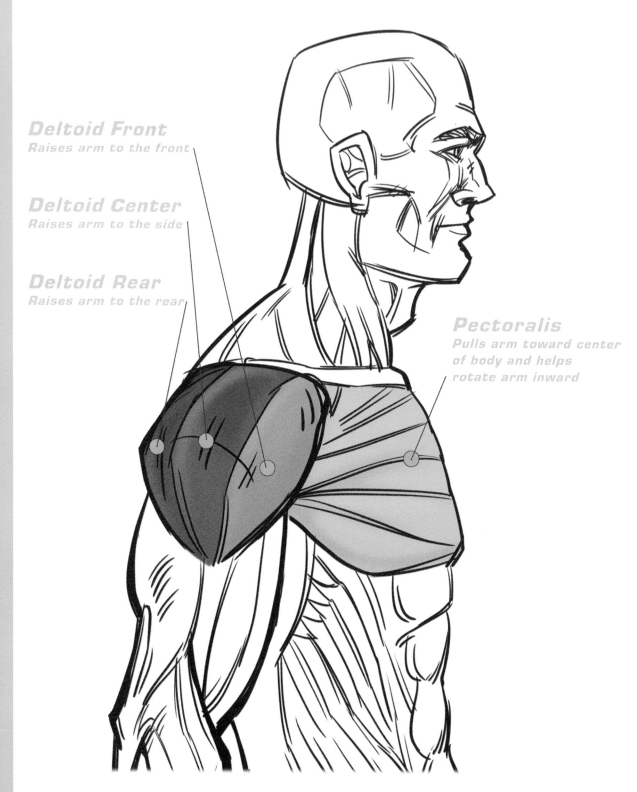

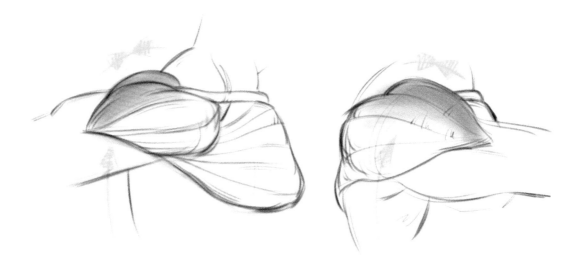

In the side view, we can see how the CONTRACTION of the front and back of the deltoid decides if the deltoid region will lift the arm to the front or rear of the body.

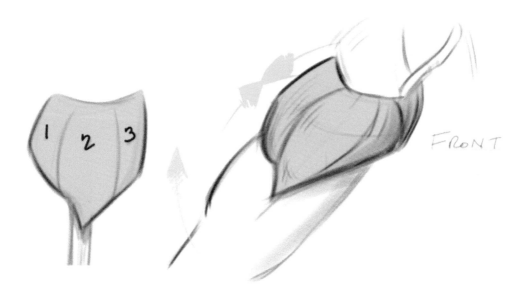

FRONT

Be mindful of the shape of the deltoid. Make certain that the shape reflects the function the deltoid is performing. Above, we can see how the deltoid front is stretched due to the arm being raised backward. This creates CONTRACTION in the rear and stretch along the front.

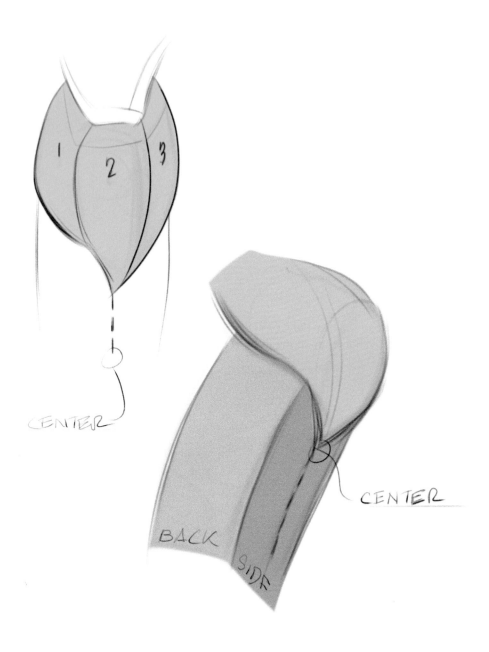

Paying attention to the concept of centering will help throughout the entire figure; one area I use this idea most is in the arms.

The lowest tip of the deltoid is centered along the outside surface of the upper arm. Awareness of this idea and using it, quickly brings form to the arm and sets up many of the other muscles found in the arm.

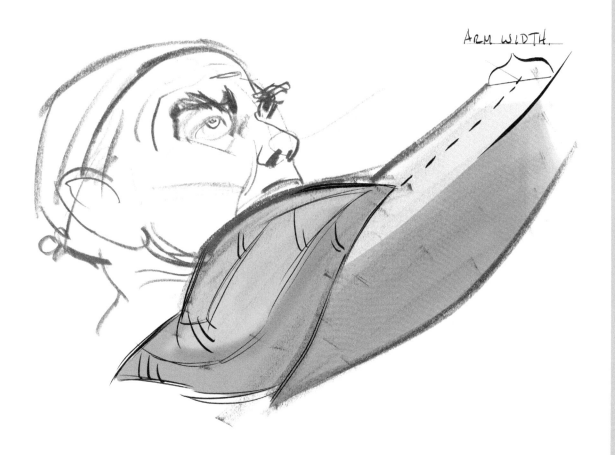

ARM WIDTH.

Here, the arm is raised due to the CONTRACTION of the center and front deltoid muscles. When I am drawing the figure, I love these views of the face. I imagine myself climbing over the surface of a mountain, the deltoid, conquering its height to reveal a 40-foot-tall monolith of a sculpted face.

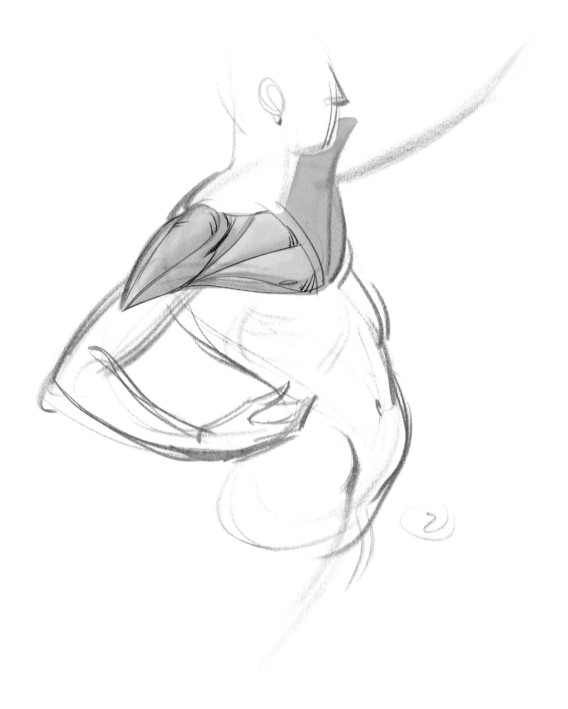

This view of the pecs and deltoids shows them stretching back as the elbow rises. In the closer arm, the rear deltoid is contracting. The pectoralis stretches from its origin, the sternum, to the humerus, its insertion.

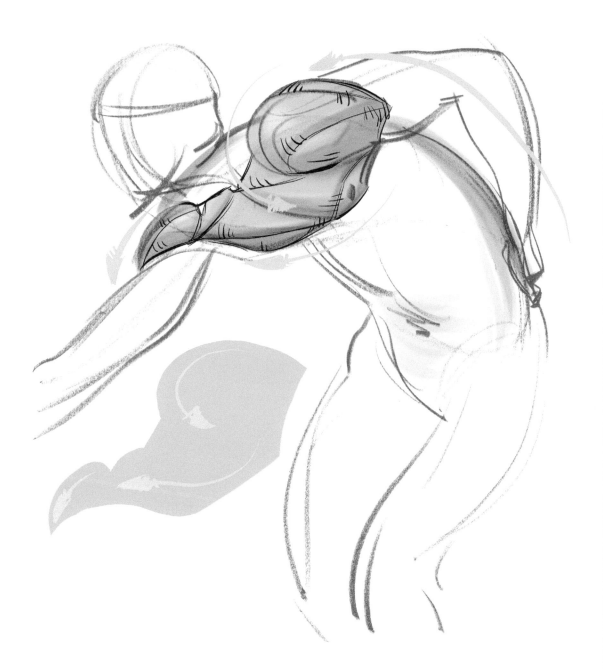

The blue arrows here show FORCE driving up the back and side of the body. This FORCE then travels through the pectorals. The pectoralis muscle on the left side of the page swings up and over the humerus bone like a claw or talon. Notice the tiny triangle of negative space between the top of the far pecs and the deltoid. Similar to the negative shape found in the sternocleidomastoid, this negative, triangular shape is a quick anatomical reference. The separate shape below shows how design emerges from the FORCES of the anatomy. The green abdomen presents the CONTRACTION found here.

EXERCISES AND TIPS

1. Practice drawing the deltoid shape and bringing the tip of it to the center of the arm's side view. Try doing this in different perspectives.

2. See how the shape of the deltoid changes based on the function it is performing.

The back is the broadest expanse of musculature in the human figure. I remember staring in confusion at the sea of indents and protrusions, wondering how I would ever understand what I was looking at. I am going to share with you my findings and process to understanding the complexities of the upper back. We'll move slowly and hierarchically to get a full understanding by looking back into the skeletal structure, the layering of the muscles, and, finally, how they function with a FORCEFUL figure. The scapula, with its family of four muscles, ends the trip of this system on the flat of the upper back.

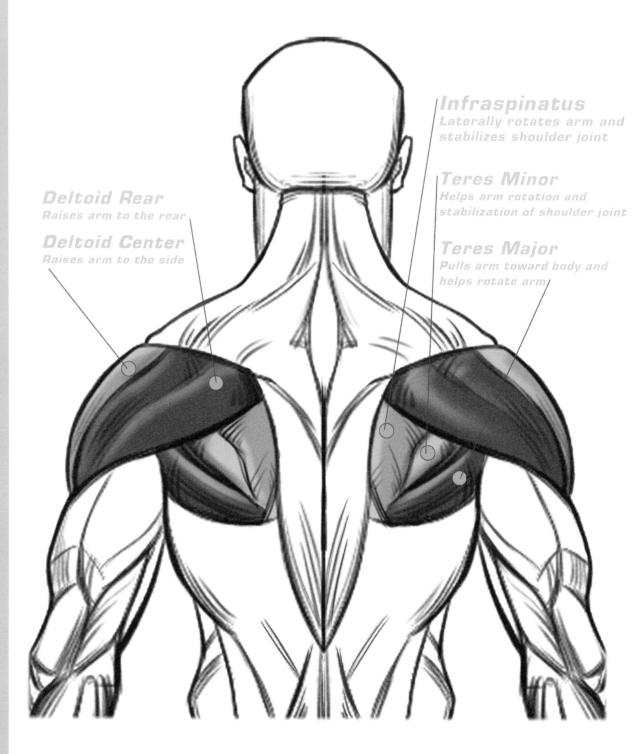

Infraspinatus
Laterally rotates arm and
stabilizes shoulder joint

Teres Minor
Helps arm rotation and
stabilization of shoulder joint

Teres Major
Pulls arm toward body and
helps rotate arm

Deltoid Rear
Raises arm to the rear

Deltoid Center
Raises arm to the side

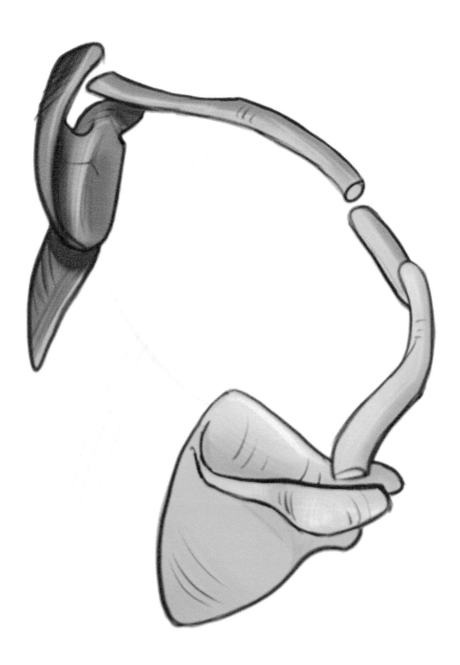

This view is of the back, in a top–down, three-quarter angle, looking at the right shoulder. See how the scapulae, the plural of scapula, rest on the surface of the rib cage. The scapulae possess a wide range of motion and have numerous muscles attached to them to support the CONTRACTIONS.

SCAPULA

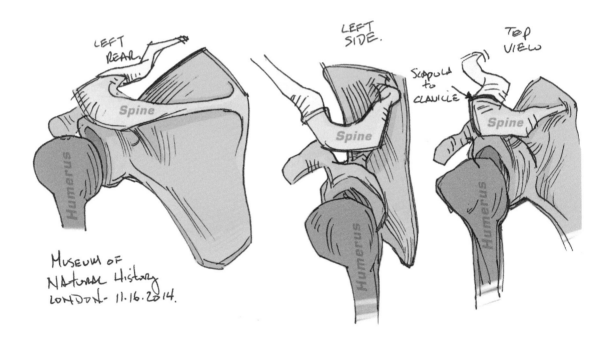

During a business trip to London, I visited the Museum of Natural History and studied some skeletons. These drawings present the scapula in different views. The humerus bone of the upper arm is dark green, and the light green region of the scapula is labeled the SPINE.

To give the arm its flexibility, a ball-and-socket joint resides under the deltoid. The humerus is the ball, and the glenoid cavity is the socket.

I must say that, in writing this book, I spent most of my time clarifying the muscles around the scapula region and trying to clarify their shapes, skeletal connections, and functions. When drawing from the model, it is difficult to transcribe what you see when looking at the scapular regions of the back.

Right scapula

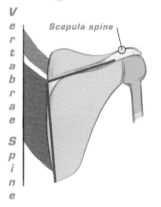

Vertabrae Spine

Scapula spine

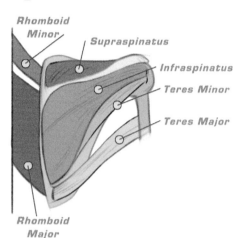

Rhomboid Minor

Supraspinatus

Infraspinatus

Teres Minor

Teres Major

Rhomboid Major

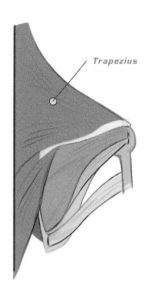

Trapezius

The three drawings above present the muscle layering of the scapula.

Left drawing: The red lines show the slightly obtuse angle created by the scapula's spine and the scapula's vertical edge near the back's spine. This important angle will be discussed further in upcoming drawings.

Middle drawing: Here, we see all of the muscles attached to this side of the scapula. Notice the opposing angles of the rhomboids relative to the angle of the muscles on the scapula. This is due to how they function when the scapula rotates. Also, see how the teres major connects to the humerus below the shoulder joint.

Right drawing: Finally, the trapezius fits over the supraspinatus and is attached to the scapula spine.

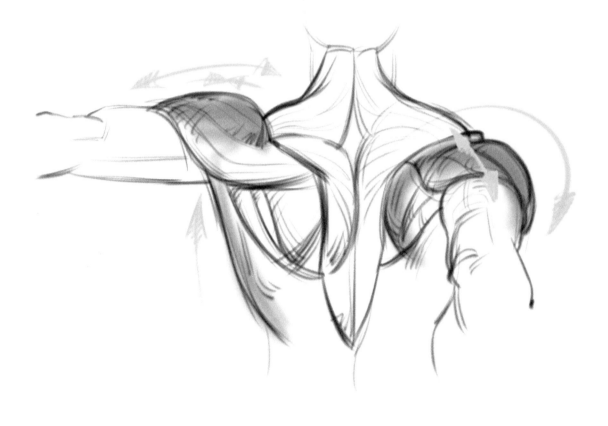

This drawing shows the two arms functioning in different ways. The left arm's center deltoid muscle contracts to cause the lift. The right arm is lifted upward toward the camera, caused by the contracted rear deltoid.

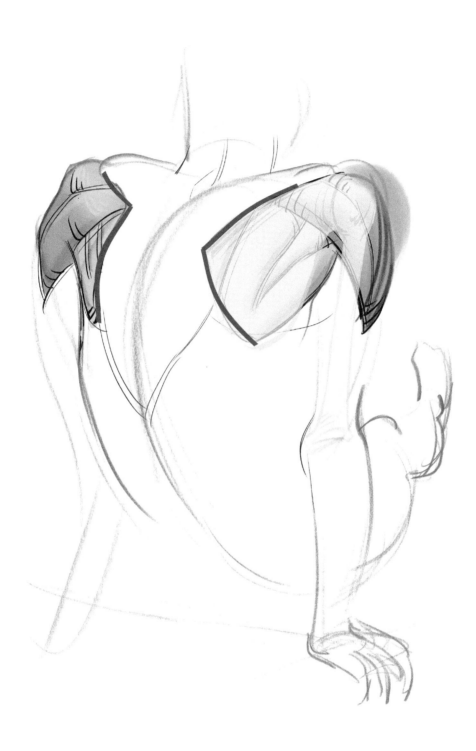

Look at the shape and rotation of the scapula and its family of muscles. These muscles then, in turn, affect the shape of the trapezius. The deltoid rests on top of it. I used red again to call out the top-inside corner of the scapulae. This angle sets up the shape of the traps. See how the humerus bone in the upper arm connects to the scapula behind the deltoid.

RHOMBOID MINOR

RHOMBOID MAJOR

This model stretches her arms upward, and therefore the bottom of her scapulae rotates away from the spine, shown with the blue arrows, stretching the rhomboids and contracting the tops of the deltoids. The rhomboids are hidden underneath the trapezius muscles. The red lines are the markers that I use from the scapulae when drawing the back.

With this final drawing, you can see the edges of the scapulae used to further describe the round form of the back. These lines show us how the back is similar to a ball-like form, just like the examples of the surface lines shown in Chapter 2.

EXERCISES AND TIPS

1. Start by drawing flat-shaped diagrams of the back's regions. Start with the following:

    a. *Shoulder blades*—Find the top ninety degree angle of the inner shoulder blade. Then, use this information to help define the trapezius.

    b. *Trapezius*—Connect it to the base of the skull, the far corners of the shoulders, and drop the dagger shape down the spine.

2. Try applying these flat regions to figure drawings, presenting the back in all different angles and functions.

3. Then, add form to the muscle, shape map.

The arm's functions are based around the shoulder's ball-and-socket joint and the elbow hinge joint. The elbow supports two processes: (1) bending, which shortens the distance from the hand to the shoulder and (2) the rotation of the forearm and thus the wrist and the hand. There are many muscles in the lower arm, and I divide them into groups based around the ulna. One keynote in this view of the lower arm is how the biceps divide the lower arm into halves. This view of the arm is primarily composed of the flexor muscles, those that bring the hand, the wrist, and lower arm up toward the shoulder.

Deltoid
Raises arm up away from body
and rotates it

Triceps
Extends forearm
at elbow

Biceps
Raises lower arm
to upper arm

Brachialis
Flexes forearm
at elbow

Brachio Radialis
Flexes forearm at elbow

Pronater Teres
Turns and flexes arm

Flexor Carpi Radialis
Brings hand up to forearm

Palmaris Longus
Flexes hand

Flexor Digitorum Superificialis
Abduction of wrist and thumb

Abductor Pollicis Brevis
Abduction of wrist and thumb

Extensor Carpi Radialis Longus
Raises top of hand to forearm

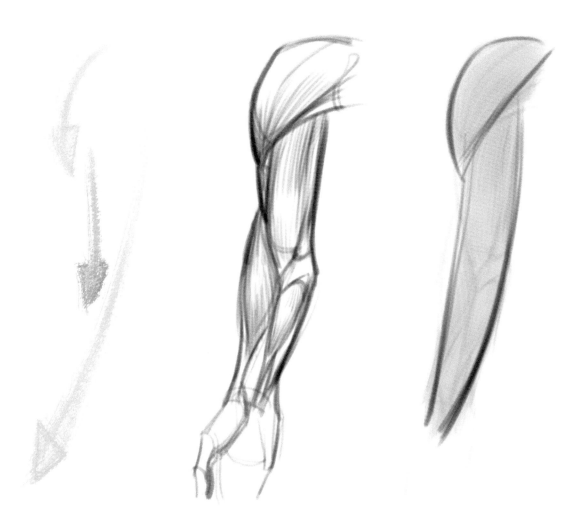

In this three-step visual, you can see how simple the FORCE and the shape steps are. The complex anatomy rests within these steps. The simplicity allows you to keep function in mind first and see how rhythm flows out to the hand.

In general, this side, the front of the arm, is where the flexors reside. This means that the CONTRACTION of the flexors curls the wrist toward the upper arm. When we reach the rear view section of the arm, the extensors will be the primary muscles in lifting the top of the hand toward the upper arm.

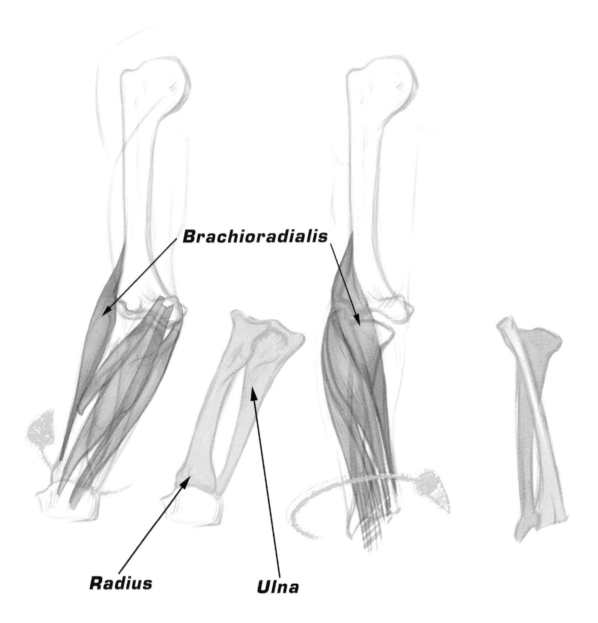

Brachioradialis

Radius

Ulna

The radius bone rotates over and around the ulna. It is this two-bone system in the lower arm that allows for the rotation in the wrist. You can see the brachioradialis rotate over the radius bone. Also, notice here where the tendons of the muscles connect and how they move over the elbow joint and, in some cases, the wrist.

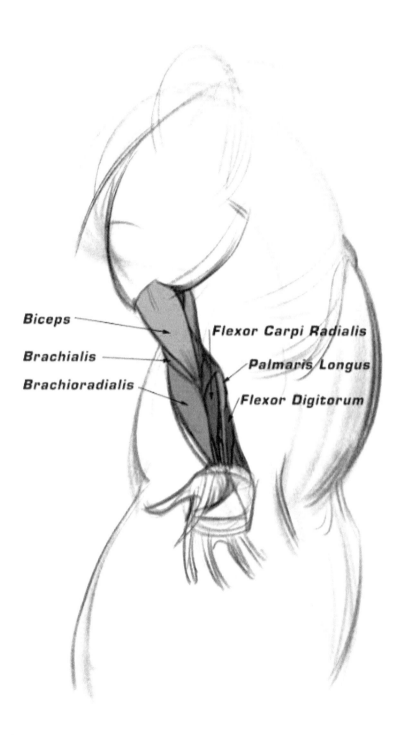

Biceps

Brachialis

Brachioradialis

Flexor Carpi Radialis

Palmaris Longus

Flexor Digitorum

This drawing demonstrates the centered bicep dividing the muscles of the forearm in half at the inner elbow. This split then works its way on an angle toward the thumb side of the wrist. The flexor digitorum is the main muscle for curling the wrist and the majority of the fingers to create a curled fist.

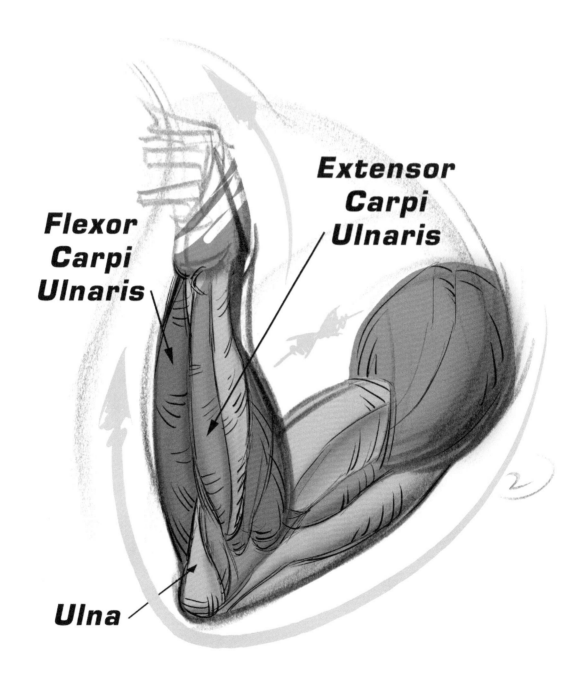

Flexor Carpi Ulnaris

Extensor Carpi Ulnaris

Ulna

The arm performs numerous complex actions in this pose. First, the bicep contracts to bring the forearm upward. Then, the muscles in the forearm rotate the wrist and the hand. You can also see how the DIRECTIONAL FORCES move through this motion. In this view of the forearm, I use the ulna as the divider of the front and back muscles. The two ulnaris muscles hug either side of the ulna.

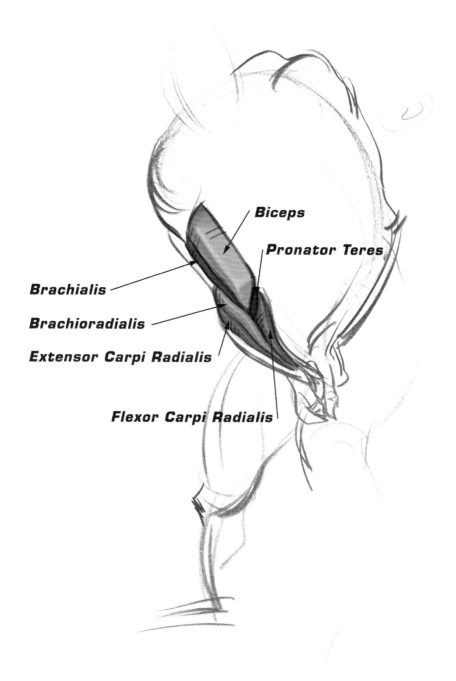

Biceps

Pronator Teres

Brachialis

Brachioradialis

Extensor Carpi Radialis

Flexor Carpi Radialis

You can see how the upper arm muscles, the biceps, and the brachialis dive down into the center of the lower arm connecting to the bones of the lower arm and bridging the elbow joint.

The upper arm is like a sandwich. The biceps are the top bun; the triceps are the bottom. The brachialis is the center of the sandwich. I use this analogy because you can see the brachialis poking out on the outside and inside surfaces of the upper arm.

Coracobrachialis

Triceps

Brachialis

Here, we can see how the CONTRACTION of the biceps lifts the forearm. The biceps is the primary contractor or flexor of the elbow joint. Remember that the origin of the biceps resides at the top of the humerus, actually attached to the scapula. Then, the muscle moves across the elbow joint and then inserts into the radius bone. Since the muscles connect across a joint, that means that, when the muscle shortens, it lifts the forearm.

Notice that the brachialis is evident here, as well as the outside surface of the upper arm, as seen in the prior drawing supporting the sandwich idea.

HAND—PALM SIDE

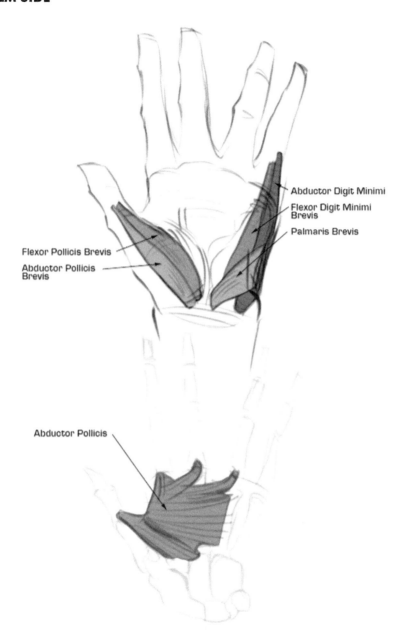

Abductor Digit Minimi

Flexor Digit Minimi
Brevis

Palmaris Brevis

Flexor Pollicis Brevis

Abductor Pollicis
Brevis

Abductor Pollicis

The hand is a complex system of anatomy furthering how we express ourselves and allowing us to perform extremely complex functions. When drawing hands, I think of the hand and the fingers like an army. When drawing hands, think about what the hand is doing. All the intricate parts work in unison performing ONE function.

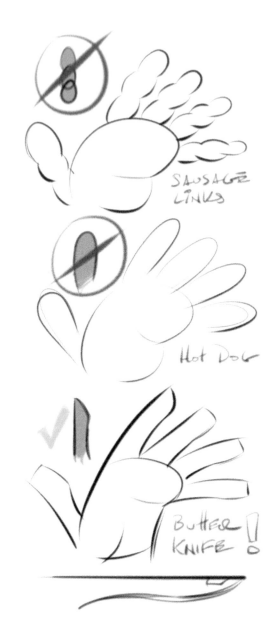

Darn fingers, how to draw them? The key is to stick with the rules of shape in Chapter 3. Above are two of the traps I see artists fall into. The sausage and the hot dog are the two foods you want to watch out for. Instead, go for the butter knife. The butter knife analogy functions the way the finger does with its gentle convex curve in the fingertip and straight top where the fingernail resides.

Another way to think about curves and straights within the hands is based on the hand's functions. The palm side is soft for caressing (curved) and grabbing. The top side is rock hard (straight) for attack and defense.

This hand gently rises, presenting the palm. This action occurs due to the CONTRACTION of the flexor muscles on the back of the forearm. FORCE comes from the arm with the focus of APPLIED FORCE at the bottom of the hand. It then moves over the top of the hand and fingers and finally shoots out the fingertips.

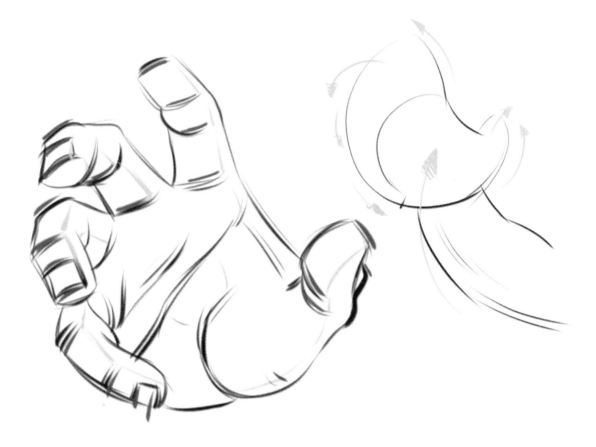

Notice in the simplification drawing, the shape that I used to connect all the fingers. The red lines represent the importance of perspective while drawing hands. Each digit must be parallel with the other digits within a given finger. This concept is presented in the image on the left with the red lines. This is easy to draw incorrectly, and, when it happens, the fingers look broken. Ouch!

EXERCISES AND TIPS

1. Remember to use the biceps to split the top end of the lower arm's muscles. This split move diagonally across the forearm to the thumb side.

2. Pay attention to the location of the ulna and how the radius bone rotates over it.

3. Draw the hands, seeing the simple shapes first.

4. Pay attention to the parallel perspective moments within each finger.

In the side view of the arm, the biggest challenge lies in seeing the simplicity of the **FORCEFUL** function and how it connects to the shoulder and the body. Drive rhythm through the arm and the hand and out of the fingertips. Here, the subtle inversion of the hand can create an extra rhythm. The centered anatomy of the upper arm is where the forearm muscles then emerge, moving over the elbow joint and creating the rotation potential of the lower arm. The carpal bones that create the wrist connect the hand to the forearm.

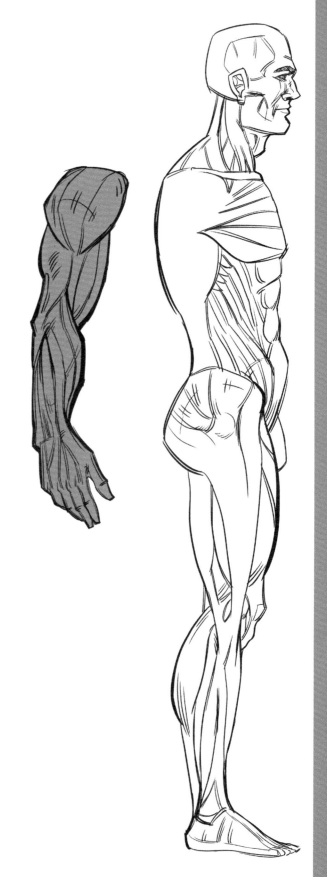

Deltoid
Raises arm up away
from body and rotates it

Biceps
Raises lower arm
to upper arm

Triceps
Extends forearm
at elbow

Brachioradialis
Flexes forearm at elbow

**Extensor Carpi
Radialis Longus**
Extension and abduction of
the wrist

Brachialis
Flexes forearm
at elbow

Anconeus
Turns and flexes arm

**Extensor Carpi
Radialis Brevis**
Extension and abduction of
the wrist

**Extensor
Digitorum**
Extension of
the wrist,
raises top of hand

**Abductor Pollicis
Longus**
Abduction of wrist and thumb

**Abductor Pollicis
Brevis**
Abduction of wrist and thumb

**Extensor
Carpi Ulnaris**
Raises and lowers the wrist

EXTRAS

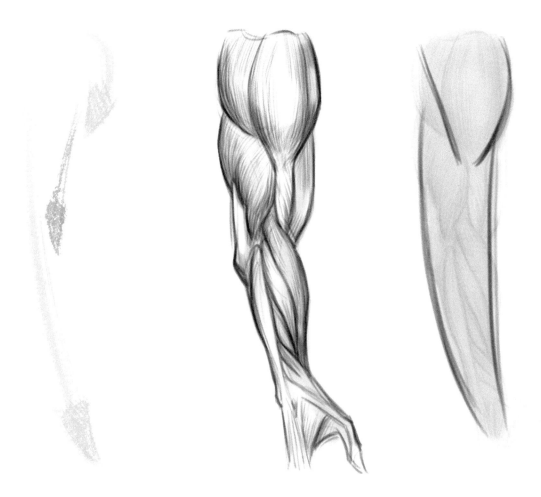

Above are the FORCE, form and shape phases of drawing the arm in the side view. Try using all of these concepts while drawing.

The brachialis muscle, found under the bicep, reveals itself on BOTH sides of the upper arm. Similar to a sandwich, the brachialis muscle resides between the two slices of bread: the triceps and the biceps.

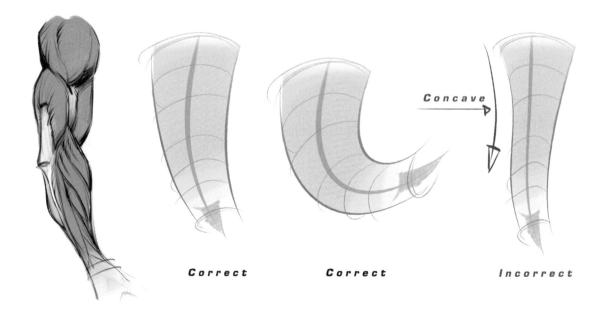

Correct   Correct   Incorrect

Notice the simplification of form described with the elliptical surface lines on the pinched tube that represent the arm, you can see the bend of the arm and the simple curvature of the arm's FORCE to execute this flexion. In this case, the bicep would flex and bulge. **FORCE stays on the path of the simple curve.** When the triceps flex as the arm is straightened, beware of the idea of placing a concave FORCE curve at the upper arm. This curve does NOT exist due to the arm's anatomical function. You will never find Directional FORCE on the bicep side of the arm.

In this drawing, you can see the rhythms of the arm move into the hand and the wood-like construction of the wrist. This simple construction helps clarify the complex surfaces of the lower arm.

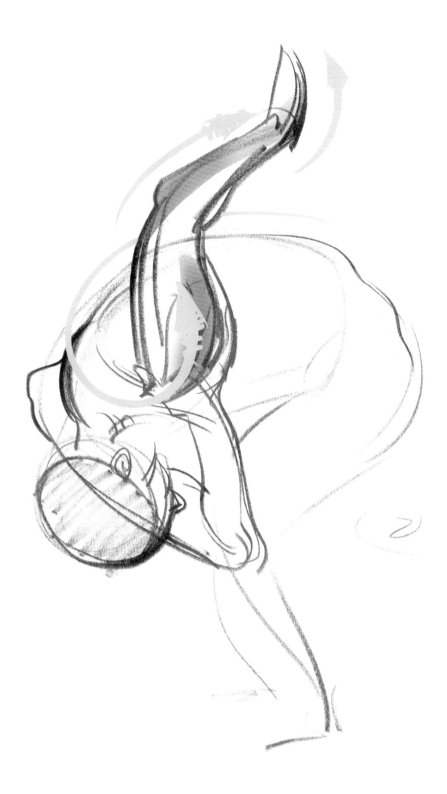

Here is a figure showing FORCE coming from the back and entering the arm. Notice the design of the arm with its straight-to-curve or FORCEFUL shapes. I see this pose as a wound-up spring. As the arm moves further counterclockwise, more energy is stored to unwind the arm's location relative to the body.

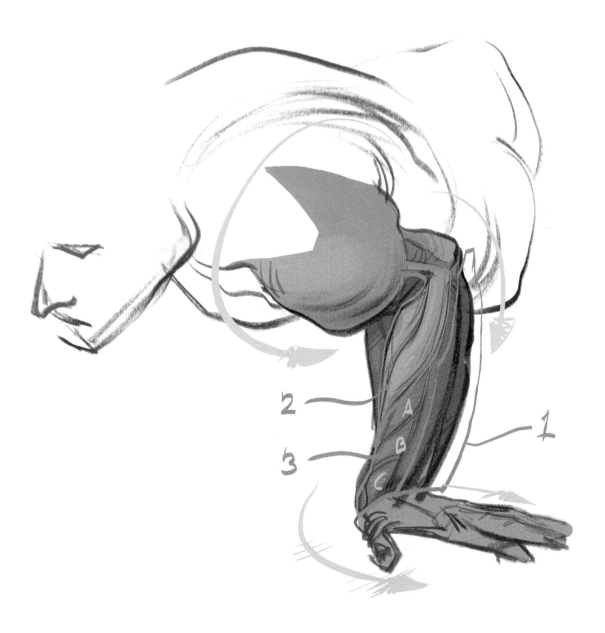

This pose has a ton of FORCE pushing into the deltoid that gets driven into the back of the upper arm and then down into the forearm and the hand.

I bracketed the three major areas of the forearm back and side:

1. The back region of the forearm, all of the extensor muscles.

2. The grouping of the brachioradialis and the extensor carpi radialis longus.

3. The last section of three muscles, from the top down:

    a. Extensor carpi radialis brevis

    b. Abductor pollicis longus

    c. Abductor pollicis brevis

The deltoid pushes upward into the body as the triceps contract, allowing for the arm to support the weight of the body. Again, I have bracketed the two groups of muscles I use when drawing the forearm from this view.

HAND—SIDE VIEW

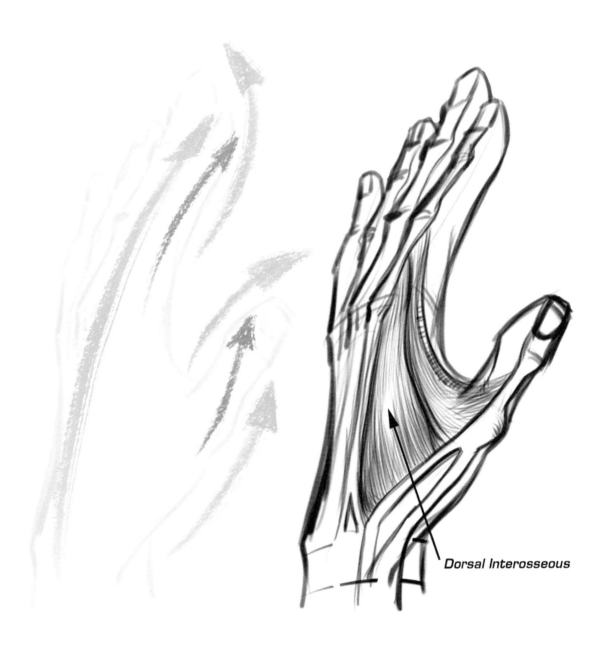

Dorsal Interosseous

This basic profile of the hand presents some of its simple anatomy and the main Directional and Applied FORCES.

The hand is one of the most complex systems in the figure, yet, it too, can be broken down into a simple, FORCEFUL shape. See this pose and how the FORCE shape of the hand can then be filled with anatomy and form. In animation, this shape is called the "mitten." Basically, you group the fingers together along with the palm of the hand and add the thumb.

FORCE must come from the arm though and lead into the hand, through the wrist. For the hand to rise like this, the muscles on the backside of the forearm must contract. The muscles we discussed in this section are stretched.

Here is another example of the straight-to-curve shape within the hand. Look at the path FORCE takes down the thumb to its tip. I often draw the hand without the thumb as a first pass and then add it later.

Here, once more, you can see the power of "the mitten." The thumb was added afterwards, protruding from the core shape of the hand. Look at all the work I put into seeing the forms of the hand using the surface lines.

I really enjoy the simple shape of this complex pose. The idea to see is the FORCE over the top of the hand and how it drives down to the pointer finger to pinch against the effort of the thumb. I also added gray lines to show the turning edge in the fingers and included red perspective lines.

EXERCISES AND TIPS

1. The brachialis runs down the center of the side of the arm, just below the tip of the deltoid. Practice using the muscle to develop the side plane of the arm.

2. Remember that the brachioradialis and the extensor carpi radialis longus are tucked in between the brachialis and the triceps.

3. Try drawing hands using the "mitten" concept. See the fingers as a group. Fingers and the hand act as one idea to be expressive and to perform functions.

The rear view of the arm shows us the muscles that extend or, when contracted, move the forearm and the hand away from the shoulder. The TRIceps extend the arm to a straight-arm position. There are three muscles, and most forget the third tricep closest to the body. Together, the muscles create the horseshoe shape that allows for an easy understanding of the rear plane and symmetry of the upper arm. In the forearm, the extensor digitorum defines the center of the rear forearm surface. Stay mindful of the elbow joint itself, how it functions, and what it looks like. The bottom of the ulna is the area of the elbow most evident to defining the look of this joint.

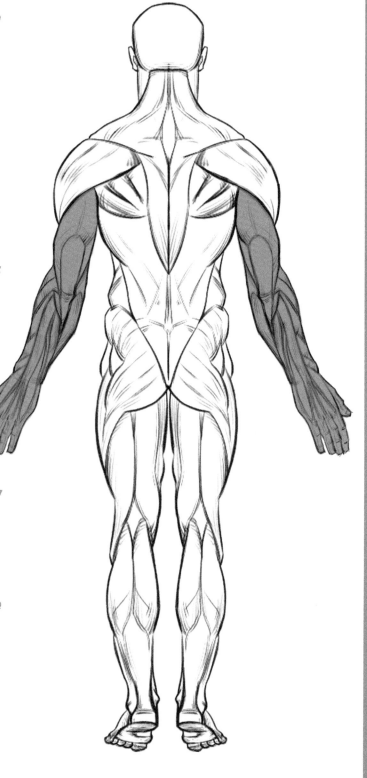

Deltoid
Raises arm up away
from body and rotates it

Triceps
Extends forearm
at elbow

Brachioradialis
Flexes forearm
at elbow

**Extensor Carpi
Radialis Longus**
Brings top of hand to
forearm and rotates wrist

**Extensor Carpi
Radialis Brevis**
Brings top of hand to
forearm and
rotates wrist

**Abductor
Pollicis
Longus**
Raises wrist
and thumb

Anconeus
Turns and flexes arm

**Flexor Carpi
Ulnaris**
Flexes the wrist,
brings palm toward forearm

**Extensor
Carpi Ulnaris**
Raises and lowers the wrist

Extensor Digit Minimi
Raises pinky or fifth digit

Extensor Digitorum
Lifts fingers and hand upward

**Abductor
Pollicis Brevis**
Raises wrist and thumb

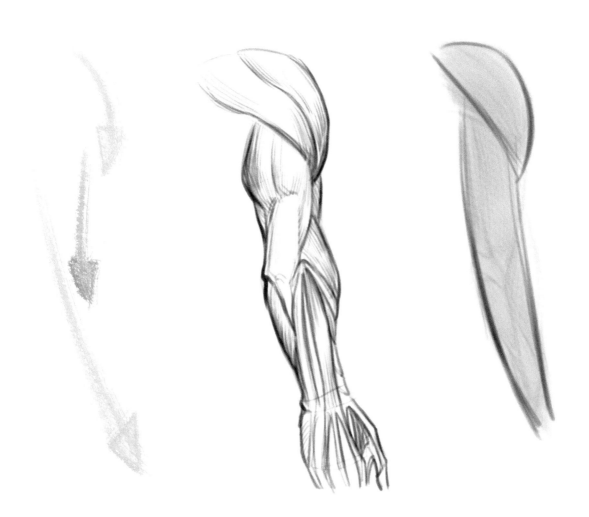

Here are the filters I see through when drawing the back of the arm. On the left, we can see the FORCES of the arm. The center shows form, basically the arm's anatomy. On the right are the arm's shapes. Notice the straight-to-curve designs.

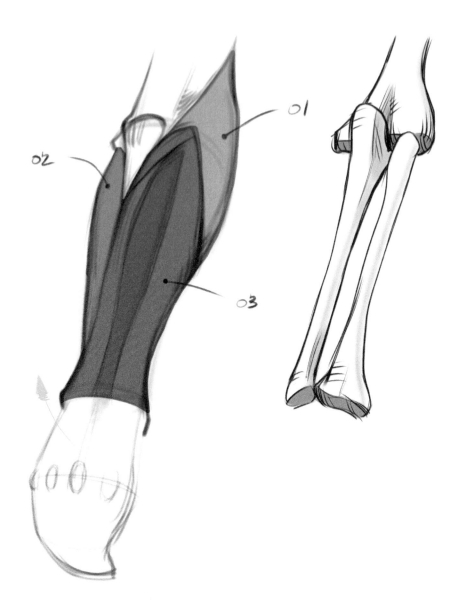

Above is a drawing of the right arm. The most complex area of the arm is the forearm. In order to simplify the amount of muscles found in this structure, I have combined muscles to create zones or groups.

Zone 01: This area helps rotate the arm. It actually consists of two muscles, (1) the BRACHIORADIALIS and (2) the EXTENSOR CARPI RADIALIS LONGUS.

Zone 02: This is the flexor area of the arm. Here, you see just the edge of the FLEXOR CARPI ULNARIS. Notice that the word flexor is at the front end of the muscle name, and at the end is ULNARIS, which is the name of the bone that the muscle is next to.

Zone 03: All the muscles here, when contracted, raise the top of the hand upward. The area is composed of the extensor muscles. The dark band in the center of this zone is the most obvious: the EXTENSOR DIGITORUM. This muscle connects to the digits or the fingers and raises them upward, extending them.

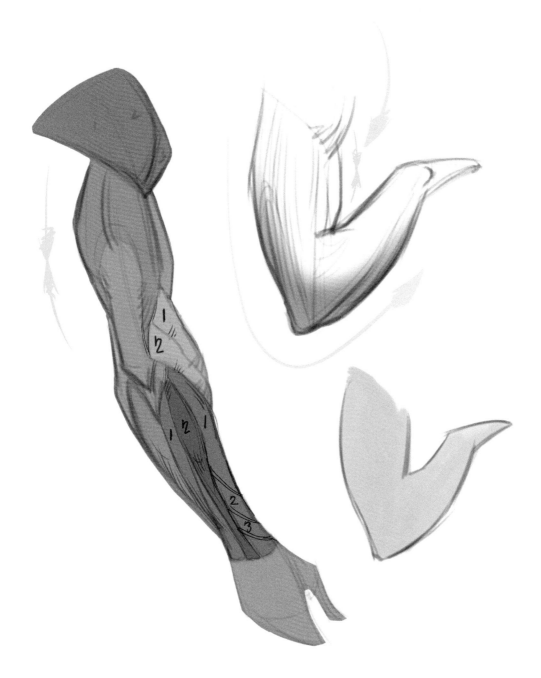

Here is a more granular breakdown of the muscles that occupy the different zones. They are not grouped and numbered by their anatomical naming but more by visual reference. This helps me remember how many muscles I want to track per area. The triceps are the primary contractor for the back of the arm helping to extend the elbow joint.

The drawing in the top right shows the Directional FORCES and the rhythm created, and green arrows show how the bicep contracts to move the arm into this position. The last image shows the shaping of the arm to combine FORCE and form.

Here, once more, you can see the separation of zones and the muscles numbered per zone. The bicep contracts here once more to raise the lower arm toward the shoulder. The deltoid does a great job of overlapping the triceps and thus, presents perspective and form.

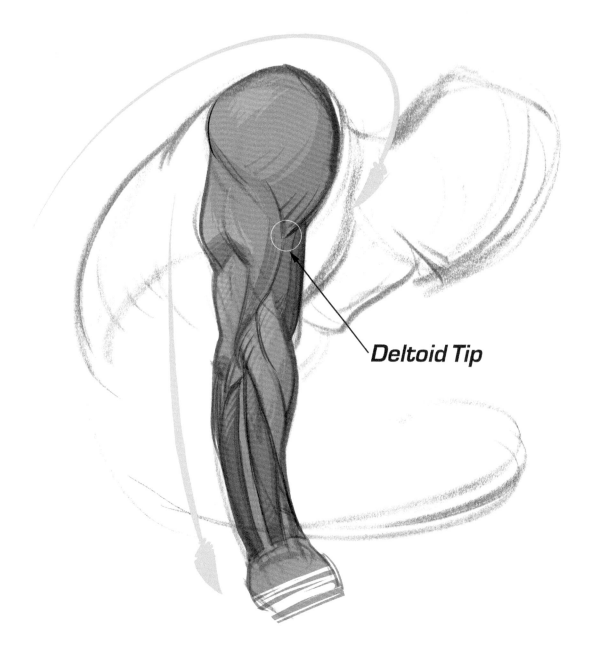

Deltoid Tip

FORCE drives up into the deltoid and then down into the column of the arm. See the triceps and the muscles of the forearm's back region. The deltoid tip does a great job here of presenting the side plane of the side of the upper arm.

Ulna

The main point of interest here is the thin black line running through the forearm area. This line represents the ulna. I use its location as a way to understand the separation between the flexor and extensor zones. In this figure drawing, you can see the contracting triceps.

Above is a page of drawings from imagination. The blue arrows present Directional FORCES, and the orange are Applied FORCES. See the common repetition of FORCE coming from the back and going into the shoulder to enter the arm.

HAND—BACK VIEW

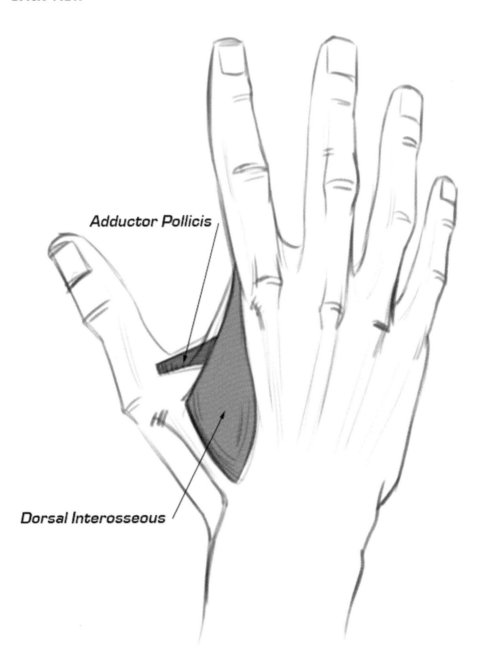

Adductor Pollicis

Dorsal Interosseous

The back of the hand shows the tendons of the back forearm muscles and how they connect down to the fingers. Keep in mind that the first digits of the fingers reside within the box of the hand itself. Then, what we know as the fingers are the last three digits.

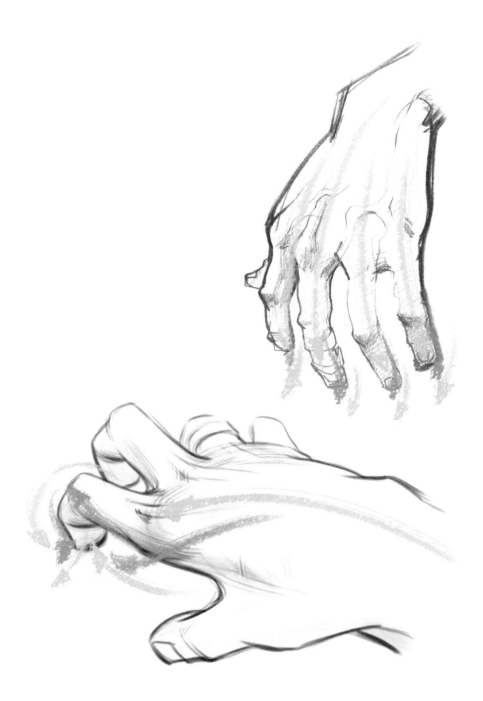

The Directional FORCE in both of these images moves over the top of the hand from the forearm. In the bottom drawing, we have an extra rhythm due to the function of the pose. Here, Directional FORCE drives down into the pad of the hand before it drives back upward into the fingers.

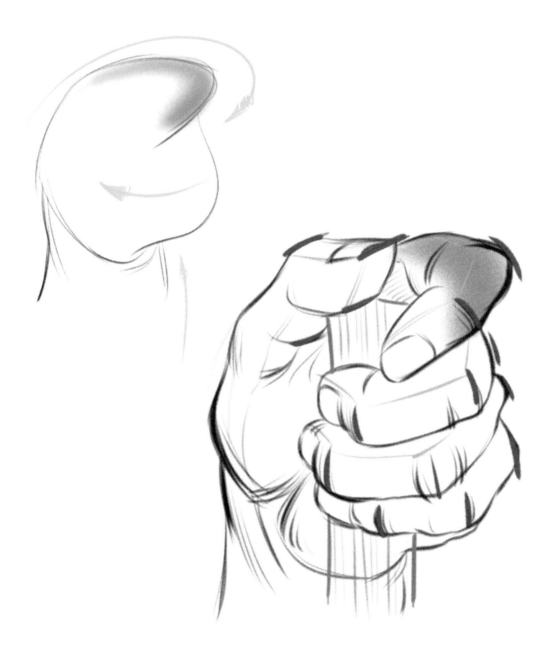

In the top-left drawing is my first impression of this complex pose. Here, on the backside of the hand, we can once again see the importance of perspective across the knuckles parallel to one another, represented in red.

Here is a great example of distilling the hand down into a simple shape. See the Directional and Applied FORCES in that simple illustration. Once more, I added the red perspective lines.

The red lines and their subtle convex and concave curves show the difference in perspective of the fingers. The first two, the pointer and the middle, come toward us, whereas the last two drop away from us. The right side or pinky side of the wrist is a straight line, whereas the thumb side is the gently sloping curve. Look at the realistic drawing; you would not know that I see the reality in these terms of simplicity first.

EXERCISES AND TIPS

1. Use the two primary tricep muscles to define the horseshoe shape of the upper arm.

2. Use the deltoid to wrap over and around the top of the triceps.

3. Use the tendons at the bottom of the forearm muscles as connectors across the top of the hand, into the fingers.

4. Use the knuckles to help place the connections of the fingers to the hand.

The amazing flexibility of the spinal column, coupled with the complexity of muscles connecting the rib cage and the pelvis, allow for multidirectional bending and rotation in the body's core. Although symmetrical in the front view, the core creates dynamic poses and contains almost half of the human body. Notice that the infamous "six-pack" is actually eight, with the top two muscles sitting at the bottom of the rib cage. From the front view, the most obvious groups of muscles are the abdominal muscles. When contracted, they allow the rib cage to move closer to the pelvis.

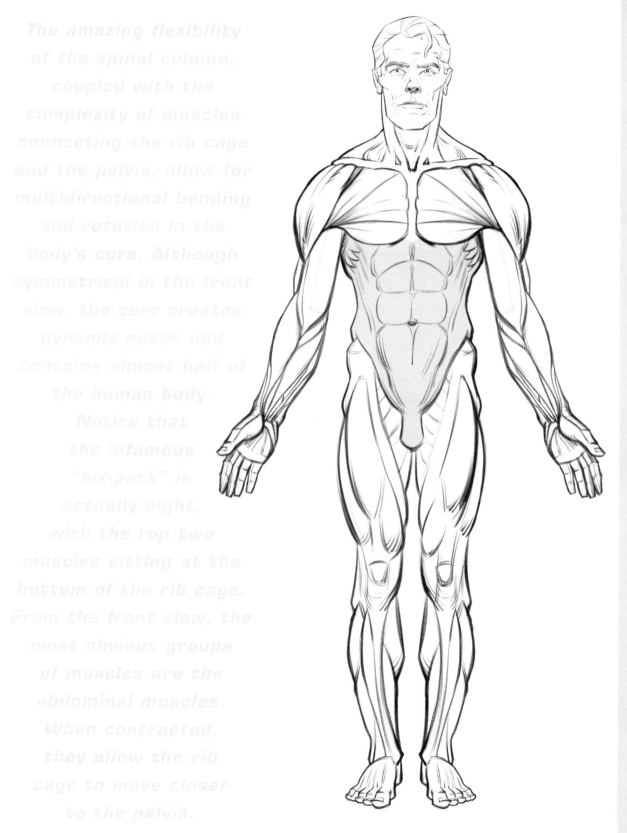

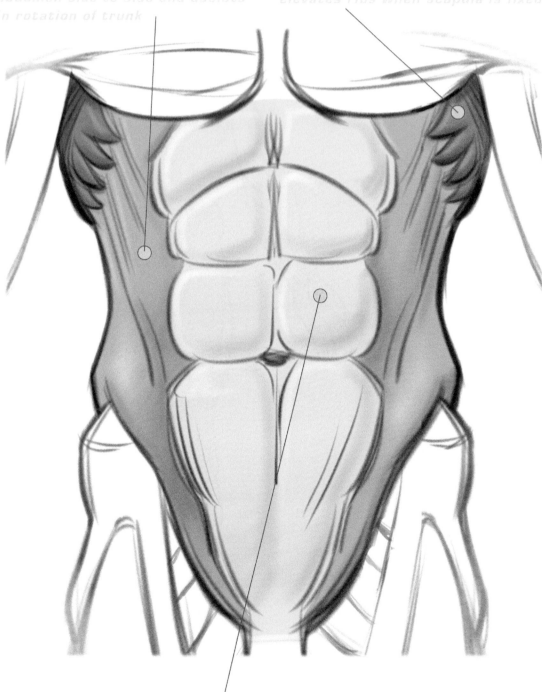

Obliques
Bilateral contraction helps bend the
abdomen side to side and assists
in rotation of trunk

Serratus
Holds scapula close to the rib cage,
elevates ribs when scapula is fixed

Abdominals
Pulls the chest to the pelvis causing
the vertebrae to stretch

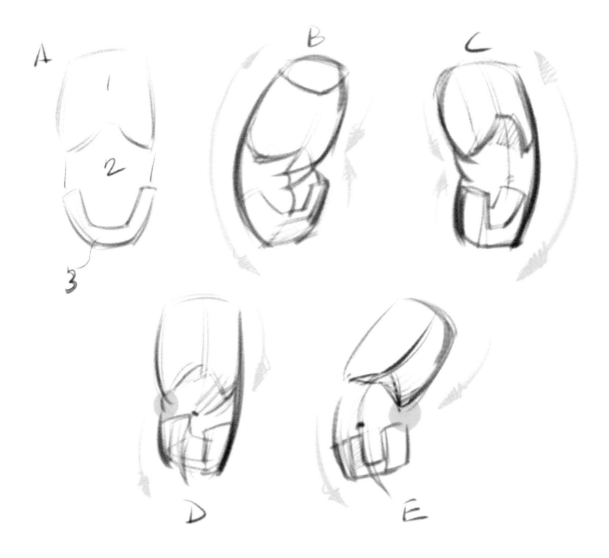

The core is the area of muscles between the hard structure of the rib cage and the pelvis. This region is composed of numerous muscles, primarily the abdomen, the serratus, and the obliques. The above drawings show how DIRECTIONAL, APPLIED, and CONTRACTION FORCES act upon these two rigid structures through bending and lateral rotations.

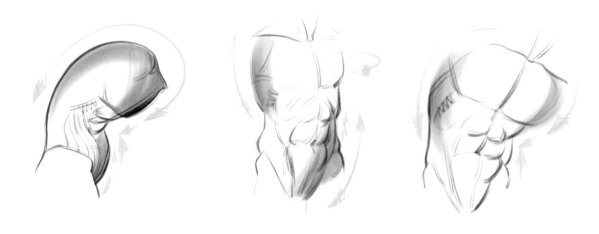

Here are more samples of similar actions with more detailed anatomy applied. Note the "C"-like FORCES in the drawing on the left.

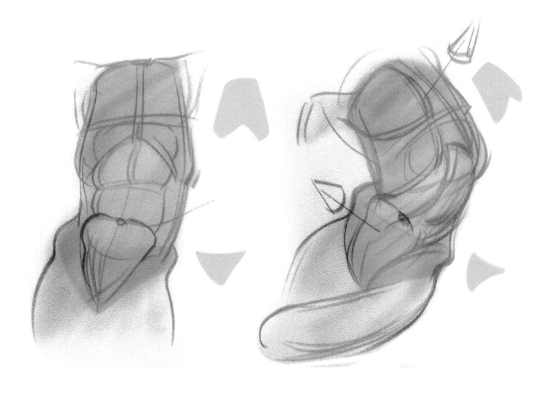

The core muscles allow the body to bend and rotate in numerous directions. It is this region that gives us torque, due to the rotation between the rib cage and the pelvis. I use the spatial direction of the navel and the sternum to help me understand how the abdomen functions between these two structures. See the shapes of these rigid forms, and try to find the straight to curves within them. The image on the left is more straightforward, and therefore the shapes of the rib cage and the pelvis are more symmetrical. On the right, the rotation helps define the FORCE shapes.

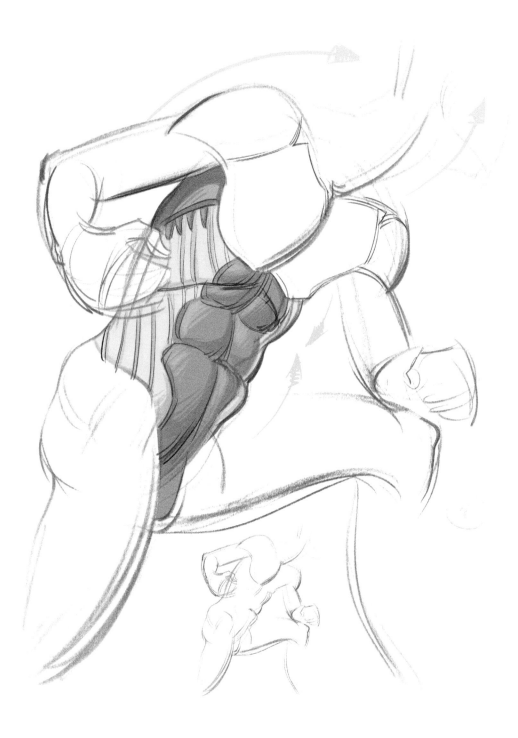

The slight tension in the abs helps hunch the body forward over the left leg. Notice in the original drawing the wrinkle of the belly to the belly button. This simple line defines the anatomy and form of the figure.

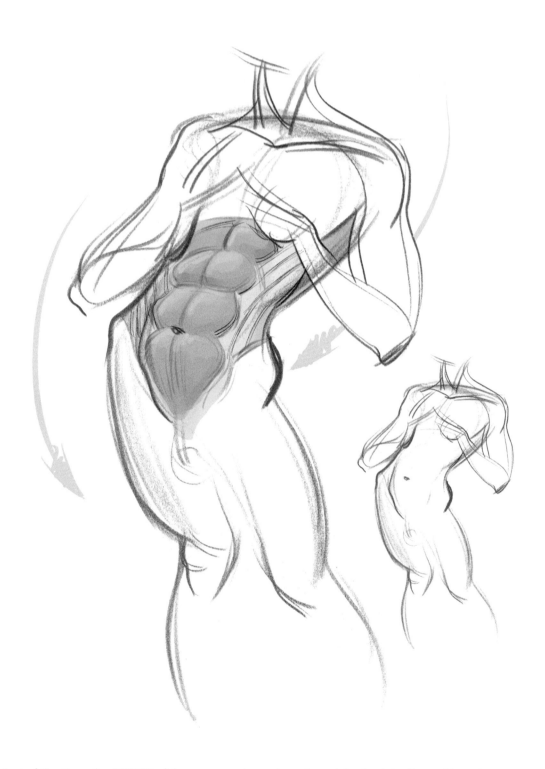

Most of the time, the FORCE of the upper or thoracic region of the back is directed into the abdomen. In the original drawing, see how I grabbed the far edge of the abdomen to define anatomy and volume.

Here is a figure drawing with its own goal written below it, "twisted torso." During my classes, I have students write what it is that they want to accomplish prior to drawing the model. This focuses the mind on a goal. As you can see above, my goal was to twist the torso.

EXERCISES AND TIPS

1. Use the navel to define the vertical start location of the bottom two abs. Then, place a line between the bottom of the ribs and the navel. This line defines the top four abs, then the last two abs or at the bottom of the ribs, just under the pecs.

2. Use the direction of the pecs and the hips to find rotation moments that create torque.

3. From the front view, the side of the body that bends is determined by the side where the obliques contract.

In the profile, you can
see how the upper back
FORCE moves across to
the abdomen. The obliques
surround the side's core.
They run along the sides
of the abdominal muscles,
attached to the rib cage,
intertwined with the
serratus. The obliques then
stretch down to the top
ridges of the pelvis. These
muscles, when contracted,
allow for rotation and
sideward bending between
the rib cage and the pelvis.
There is a second lower
layer to the obliques that
moves in the opposite
direction of the surface
muscles. These two layers
combined create great
strength in the core.
An informative area
to draw is where the
serratus and the obliques
connect to the rib cage.
This area gives me a
line that describes the
roundness of the rib cage.

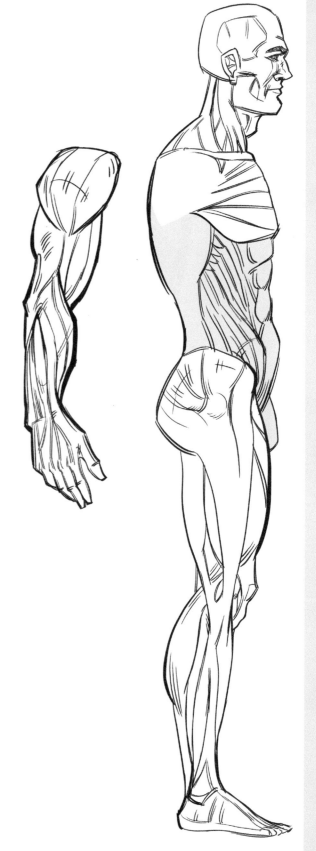

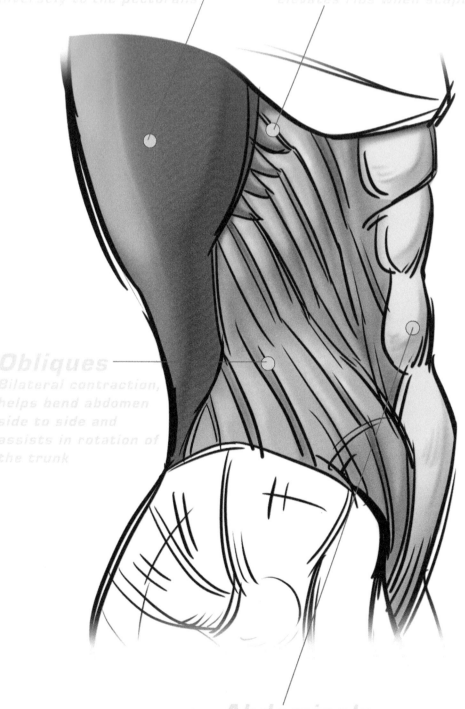

Latissimus Dorsi
Pulls arms to the body, works inversely to the pectoralis

Serratus (Serrated)
Holds scapula close to the rib cage, elevates ribs when scapula is fixed

Obliques
Bilateral contraction, helps bend abdomen side to side and assists in rotation of the trunk

Abdominals
Pulls the chest to the pelvis causing the vertebrae to stretch

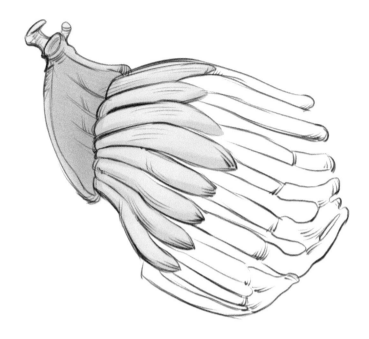

Here, I have moved the scapula out to the left to more clearly show how the serratus connects to the far-back edge of the scapula. The serratus is easy to remember because it sounds like "serrated," presenting the serrated-like edge of these muscles on the rib cage.

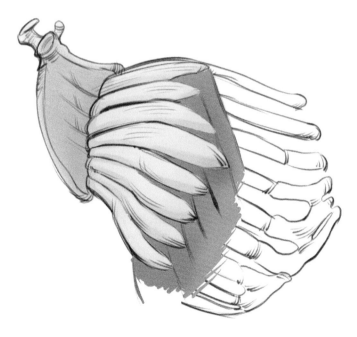

Now, we add the obliques. They are attached to the bottom of the ribs between the outreach of the serratus. These two muscle groups create an interwoven structure along the side of the rib cage. The obliques connect from the ribs down to the top of the pelvis, allowing the body to bend side to side.

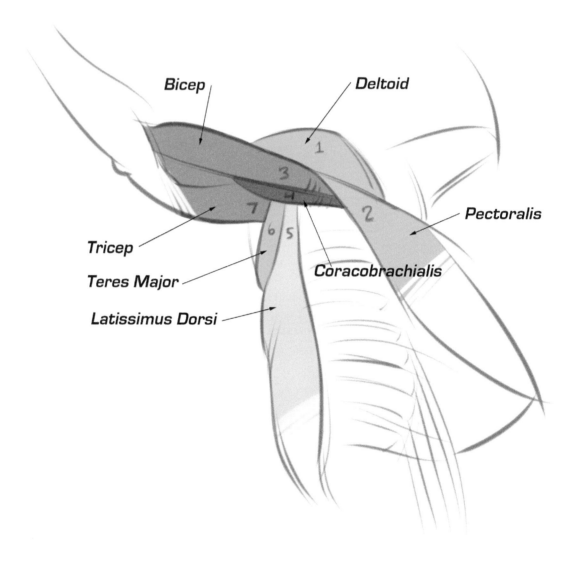

Bicep

Deltoid

Tricep

Teres Major

Latissimus Dorsi

Pectoralis

Coracobrachialis

One area of the body that always confused me was the armpit region. Here, I numbered the muscles for you in the order of overlap they create from this point of view.

The key moment here to notice is #4, the CORACOBRACHIALIS muscle, under the bicep, and how the LATISSIMUS DORSI, #5, slips in between it and the triceps to connect to the humerus bone.

TERES MAJOR is the #6, which comes from the scapula and connects to the humerus bone, right next to the lats.

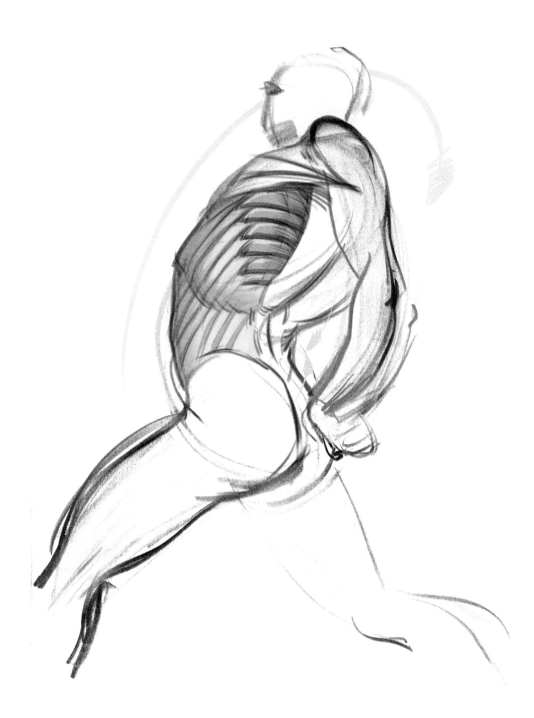

This drawing shows the Applied FORCE in the bottom of the rib cage and the CONTRACTION in the lumbar region of the back. Notice the interwoven appearance of the serratus and the obliques.

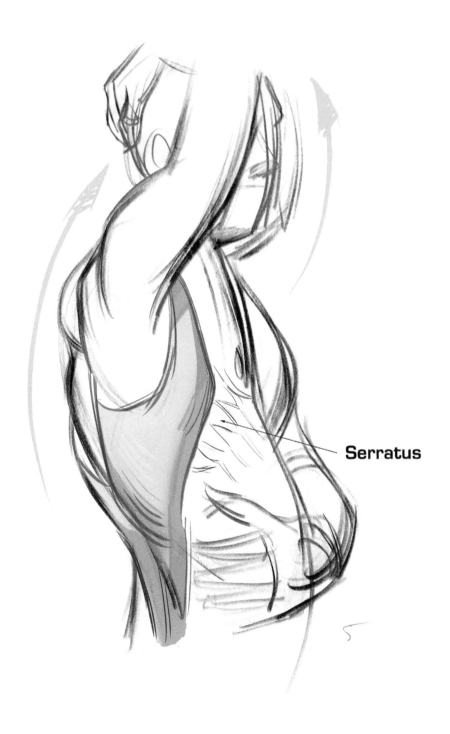

Serratus

Let's look at the lats, the last major muscle of the core. They connect up between muscles in the upper arm to the humerus, to the long edge of the spine and at the bottom to the iliac crest. The latissimus dorsi rests on top of the serratus.

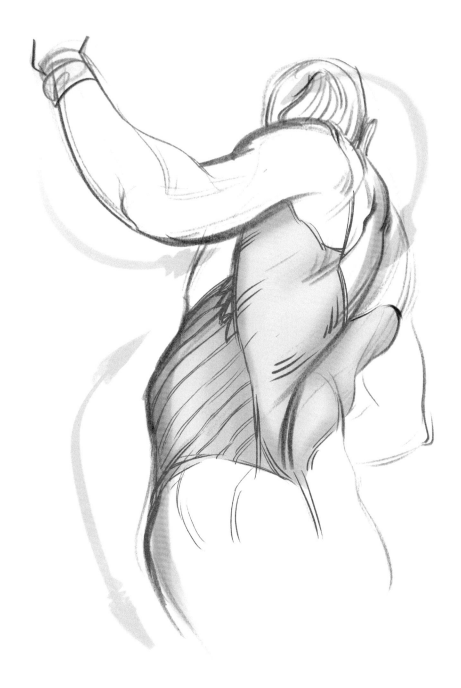

Here, you can see how the obliques wrap around the side of the body, connect to the top edge of the pelvis, at the iliac crest, and tuck under the length of the latissimus dorsi and interweave with the serratus. The serratus moves under the latissimus dorsi as well.

This final side-view drawing shows how important and useful the lats are in defining form, anatomy, and thickness. See the scapula tuck under the lats and how the lats wrap around the rib cage.

EXERCISES AND TIPS

1. Practice seeing and drawing the serratus on the rib cage and weaving the obliques in between them down to the iliac crest.

2. Keep in mind that the latissimus dorsi connects to the humerus bone in the upper arm.

3. The latissimus dorsi covers the lower tip of the scapulae.

The latissimus dorsi,
"widest back muscle,"
in Latin, assists in
pulling the arms down
to the sides of the rib
cage and arm rotation.
These muscles give
the back its fullness.
The muscles of the back
work in relationship
with those of the chest.
The lats connect to
the humerus bone,
thus contributing to
the motions of the
arm. They also connect
down to the pelvis
and to the spine.
Keep in mind that the
lower tip of the scapulae
is tucked under the lats.

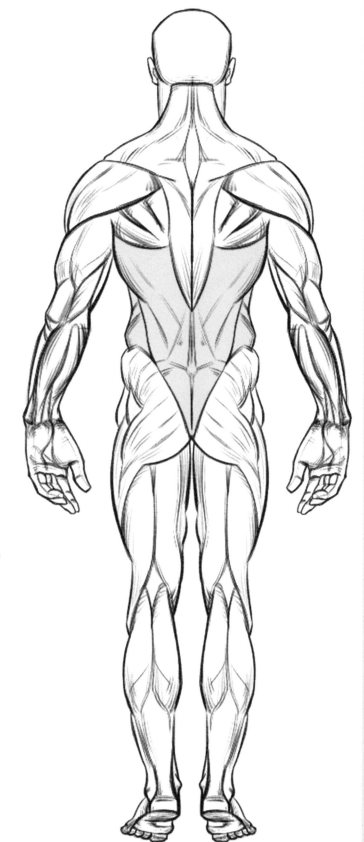

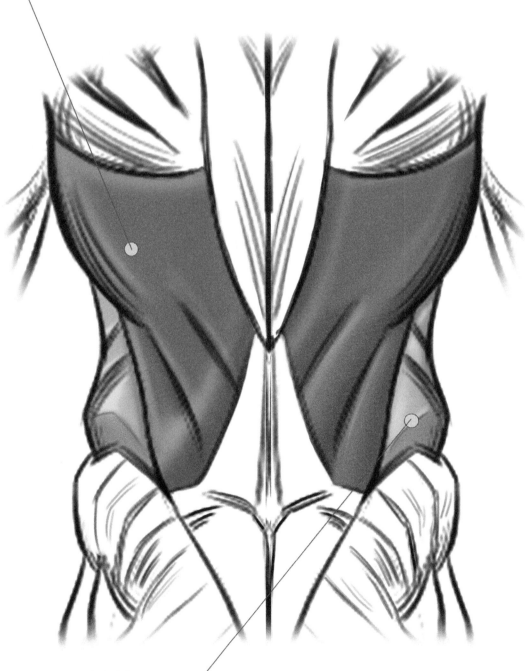

Latissimus Dorsi
Pulls arms to the body, works inversely to the pectoralis

Obliques
Bilateral contraction, helps bend abdomen
side to side and assists in rotation of
the trunk

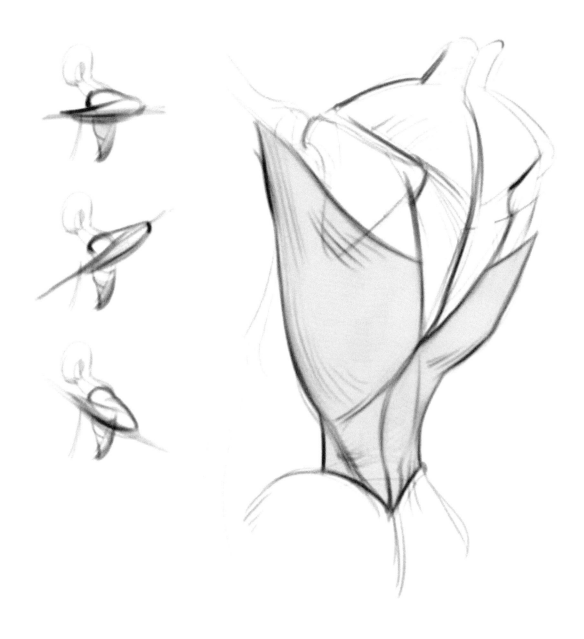

The lats help pull the arms downward to the sides of the body when contracted or pull the elbows back behind the body. This occurs because the muscle is connected to the humerus bone in the arm, along the spine, and down to the iliac crest. Think about the power this muscle can create for the arm based on its large, triangular size and its attachment to the rigid areas of the body to help pull the arms down and back. The angle of the arms when this CONTRACTION occurs determines what areas of the lats are contracting the most.

On the left, the three small drawings present how the different angles of movement affect the different areas of the lats.

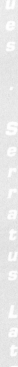

This model stretches his lats while he leans on the pole for support and balance. You can feel the pull of the lats around the bottom surface of the scapulae. Enjoy the thrill-filled ride of FORCE from the hands, down and over the upper back to the abdomen.

Here, we can feel the thick, stretched lats of the model as he sweeps his body's weight over his right leg. See the beautiful rhythms of the pose.

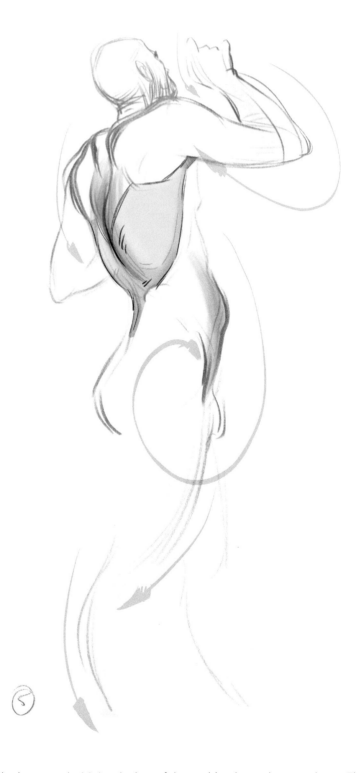

The importance of the lats to uphold the rhythm of the mid back can be seen here. The curve at the bottom of the lats on the backside directs FORCE right into the lower abs of the model. Then we can watch FORCE make its way down to the feet.

In this last figure drawing, once more, we can see the lats connected down to the pelvis with the obliques underneath, lining the side of the figure, weaved between the serratus on the rib cage.

EXERCISES AND TIPS

1. The largest muscles of the back, the latissimus dorsi, can help you define the roundness of the rib cage and help locate the bottom edge of the scapulae.

2. The obliques fill out the lower back, left and right of the lats' bottom perimeter.

The pelvis, Latin meaning, "basin," is the actual basin for the upper body. It is constructed out of four bones: (1 and 2) the two hip bones, (3) the sacrum, and (4) the coccyx. This rigid structure is our opportunity to define form for the lower region of the torso. Be aware of the pelvis box, and use the tips of the iliac crests as structure points. In the front view, I use the "v" shape of the pubis region to further define form and the direction of the pelvis. The femur connects to the pelvis through the hip joint. In this chapter, I will discuss the differences between the male and female pelvises as well. I enjoy driving **FORCE** down the side of the torso into the opposite hip, clearly defining contrapposto poses.

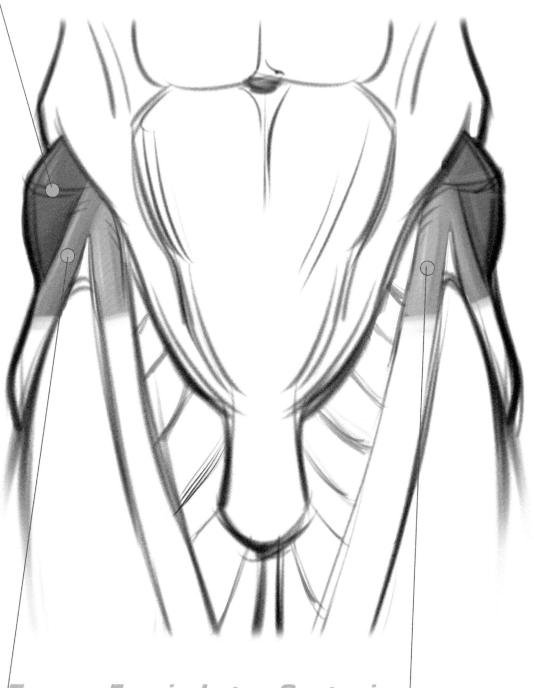

Gluteus Medius
Helps raise leg on side, stabilizes hip joint

Tensor Fascia Lata
Raises and rotates leg,
stabilizes hip and knee joints

Sartorius
Raises and internally rotates leg
at the hip joint

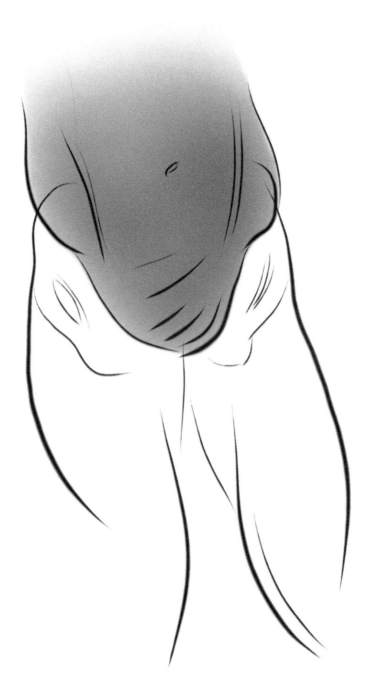

The word "pelvis" means "basin" in Latin. I like to think about the pelvis as the basin for the internal organs of the abdominal region. All this weight sits in this basin. This weight is then distributed to the sides of the pelvis, to the legs, and down to the feet.

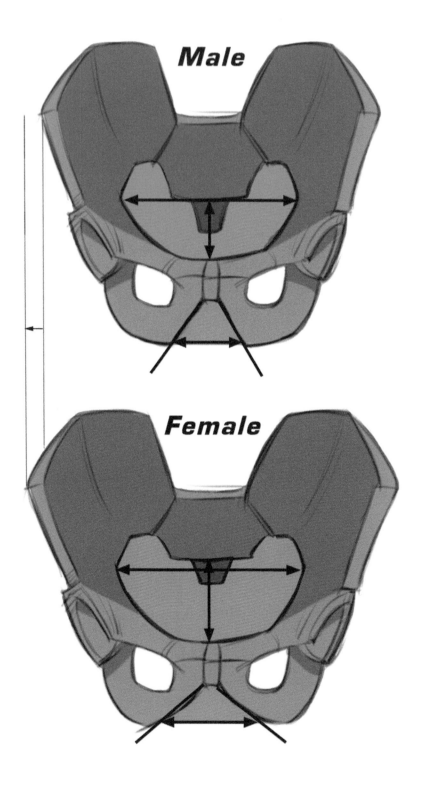

The basic difference between the male and female pelvis is defined due to function: the ability or lack thereof to give birth. The orange areas, the interior negative shape of the pelvis and the pelvis outlet, are smaller and narrower in the male than the female.

Even during a one-minute drawing, I keep in mind the presence of the pelvis. Coupled with the "v" shape to the pubic bone, shape and form are quickly and efficiently created. The shape is similar to underwear.

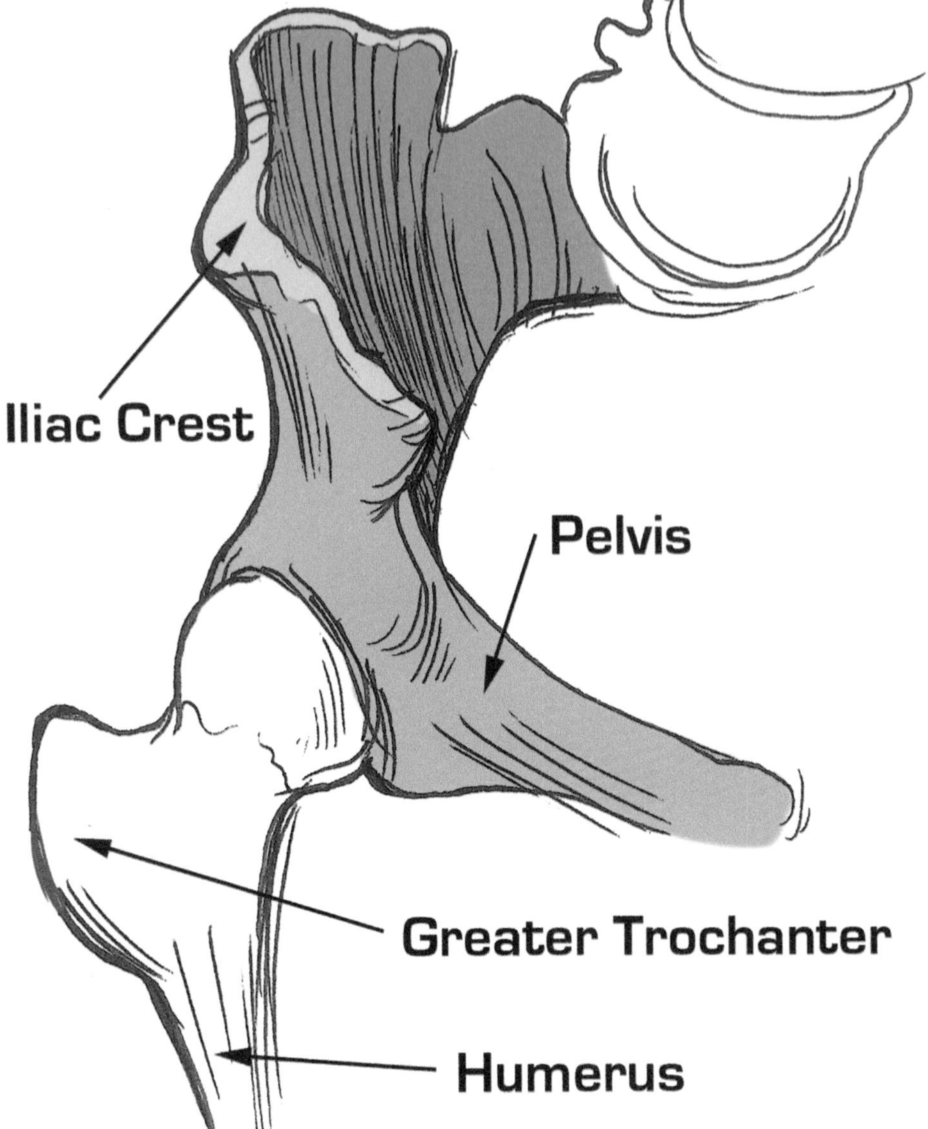

Iliac Crest

Pelvis

Greater Trochanter

Humerus

The hip joint is similar to the shoulder joint; it allows for movement in all directions. The weight of the upper body rests in this socket and gets dispersed across the structure of the pelvis. The greater trochanter is the part of the humerus that protrudes outward on the side of the leg. Many of the greater muscles of the leg are attached here.

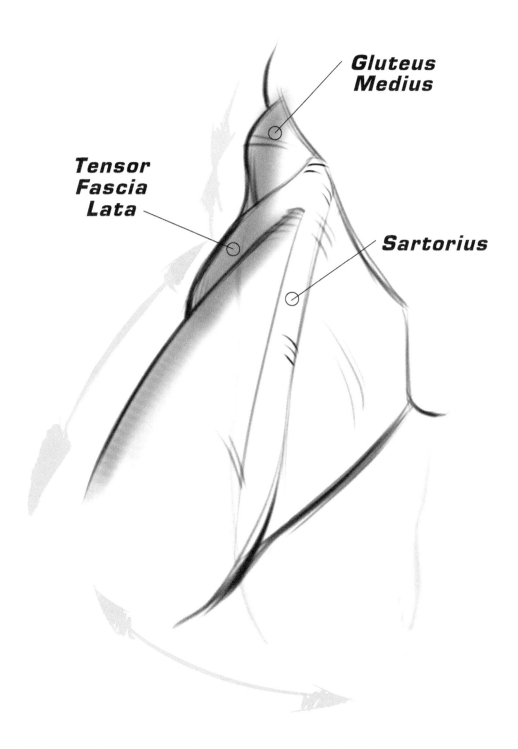

Gluteus Medius

Tensor Fascia Lata

Sartorius

Here, the gluteus medius contracts, and as it does, it supports the lateral rise of the upper leg.

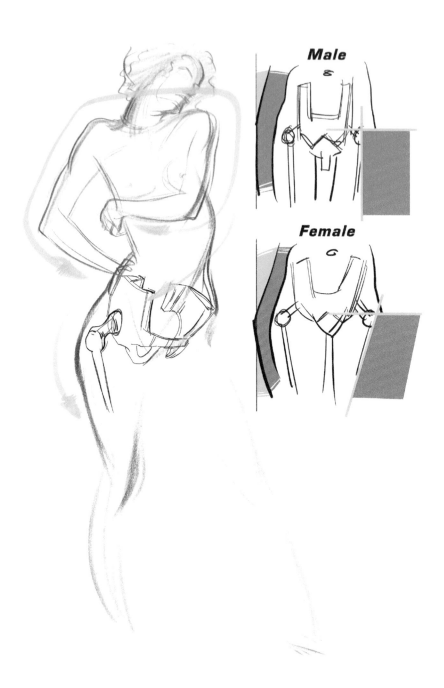

Male

Female

Above is an example of the simple construction of the pelvis. The images on the far right show the angle difference created along the outside contour of the male versus female pelvis. The female pelvis is wider than the male, so the top of the femur at the greater trochanter protrudes out further from the center of the body. Because of this, the angle down the leg from the hip to the knee is greater than the angle found in the male. This angle difference is presented with the blue lines coupled with the orange shapes.

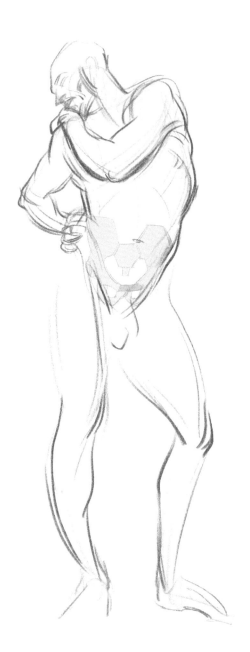

Here is the pelvis found in a male model. On the right, we see how the reverse "C" shape of FORCE is caused by the CONTRACTION of the opposite side of the figure, indicated with the green arrows.

Understanding how the pelvis is situated helps us understand the centering of the thigh and abdomen, along with the turning edge of the front to side planes of the figure. Find the belly button, find the iliac crests and the pubic bone to define clear structure along the front pelvic region of the figure.

The iliac crests are great landmarks for defining form. Since they are part of the skeletal structure of the figure, their rigidity helps define perspective. Here, you can see how the model's legs thrust outward from the pelvis, underneath the crests.

EXERCISES AND TIPS

1. Start drawing the pelvis as simple forms. Then, draw it in different perspectives.

2. Use the pelvis to create the front, side, and rear views of the figure.

3. Use the natural center of the pubic bone to align it with the navel, and see if there is any rotation in the figure.

4. Learn how the pelvis is the connector of the muscles of the torso and the upper leg.

Looking at the pelvis in the side view reminds me of its similarity to the shoulder. Instead of the deltoid muscles supporting the range of motion of the arm, we have the gluteus muscles and others to support the motions of the leg. I share with you the idea of the wrench shape in the side view and how to use it. I typically pay attention to how the obliques move over the top of the iliac crests and then dip down behind them. I also drive **FORCE** through the upper leg to the rear end, imagining where the bottom of the pelvis is and thus more accurately connecting the lower abdomen to the lower glutes. In the side view, we can also clearly see the function of the contracted gluteus maximus and the tensor fascia lata (TFL).

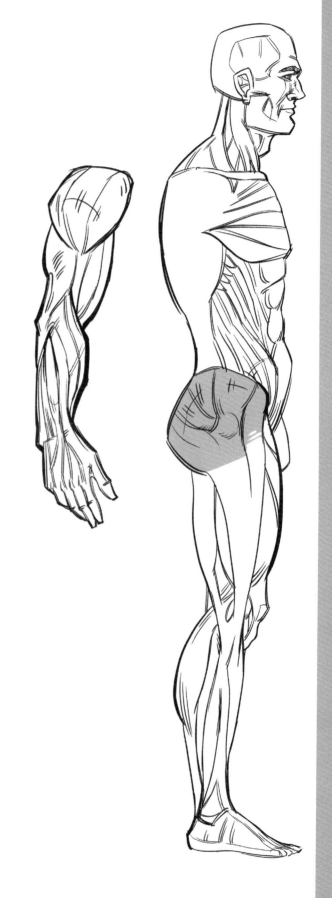

Gluteus Maximus
Helps raise leg on side, stabilizes hip joint

Gluteus Medius
Helps raise leg on side, stabilizes hip joint

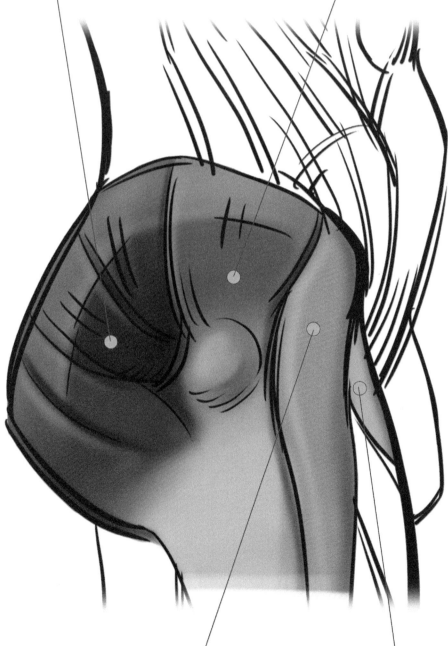

Tensor Fascia Lata
Raises and rotates leg, stabilizes hip and knee joints

Sartorius
Raises and internally rotates leg at the hip joint

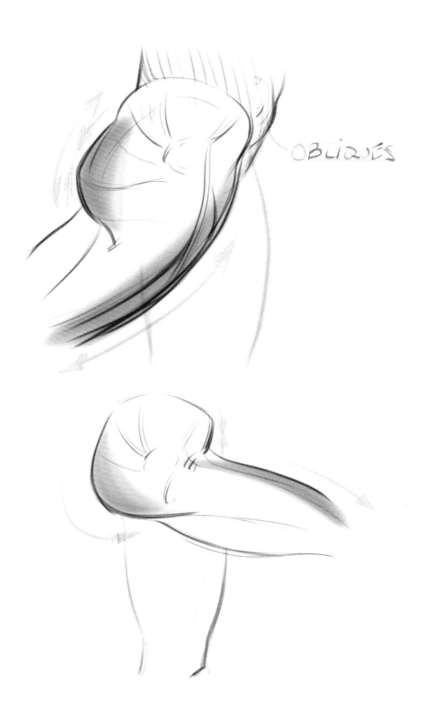

OBLIQUES

The green arrows show the contracting muscles within the pelvis region in the side view. In the top drawing, the glutes lift the leg to the rear and in the bottom drawing there are numerous muscles that contract, lifting the leg to the front of the figure. The flow of rhythm moves through the same path in either function of the pelvis muscles.

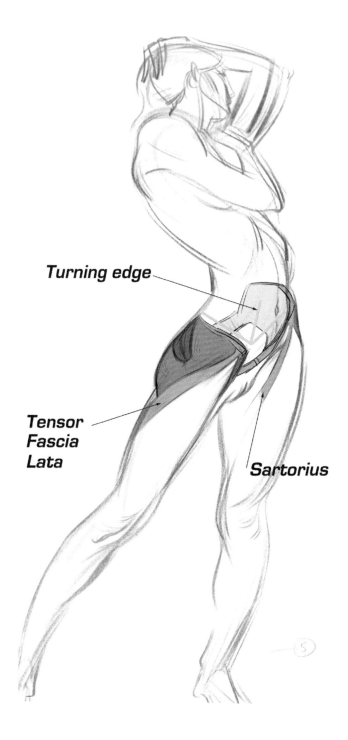

Turning edge

Tensor
Fascia
Lata

Sartorius

The blue lines call out the structural function of the pelvis or, more specifically, the front tip of the iliac crest. The blue lines show the side and front views of the body, and the vertical blue line is the turning edge. Notice that all the surface lines near the closer hip define the stretch of that area due to the leg sitting so far back.

The pelvis in the side view looks like a wrench with the hip joint in the center. Follow FORCE from the face and the neck to the upper back, over to the abdomen, and finally to the rear end.

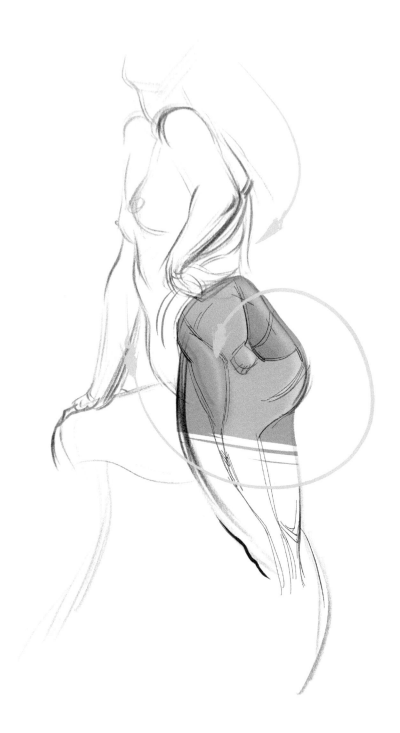

This wrench-like shape comes down from the bottom of the glutes and from the top center of the iliac crest.

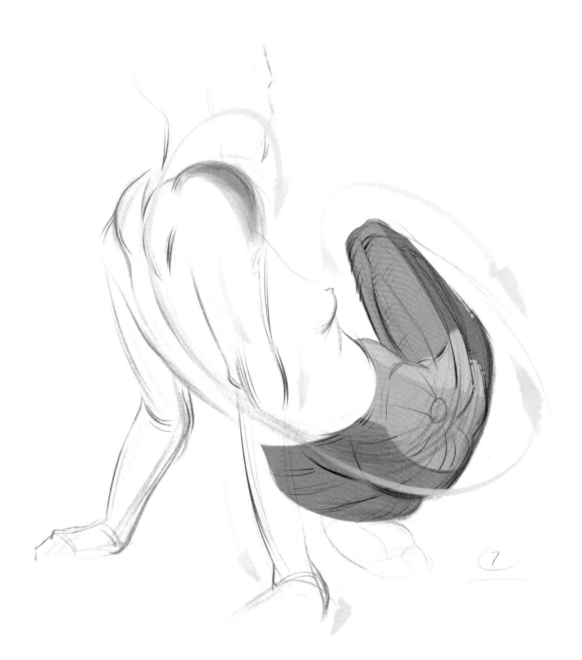

This dynamic pose shows the pelvis in a downward three-quarter view. Understanding the muscular anatomy helps me define the turning edge between the side and back of the pelvis. In this particular pose, FORCE drives down the back and over to the side of the pelvis and over to the top of the thigh.

EXERCISES AND TIPS

1. Use the hip joint and its center, the greater trochanter as a touchstone for understanding the anatomy of the hip in the side view. Think of it as the shoulder, ball-and-socket joint of the leg. From that joint, the muscles extend outward like sun rays.

2. The TFL transcends down into the iliotibial tract on the side of the leg.

3. Use the arc of the iliac crest to define the seam between the obliques and the glutes.

In the rear view of the pelvis, the gluteus maximus muscles are the most prominent of the pelvis. They are also one of the largest and therefore strongest in the figure. They connect from the coccyx and the sacrum bones across the top of the pelvis and down to the femur. The glutes help raise the leg backward and rotate it similar to the rear head of the deltoid. When drawing women, the sacral dimples and the intergluteal line, or the butt crack, create a triangle that I always use to define the perspective and surface of the lower back.

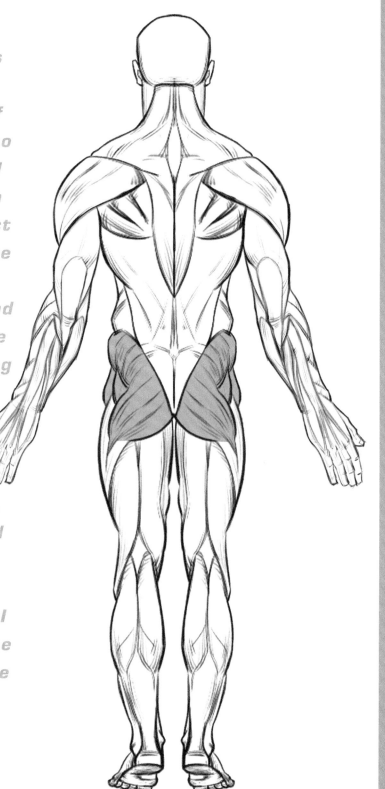

Gluteus Maximus
Helps raise leg on side,
stabilizes hip joint

Gluteus Medius
Helps raise leg on side,
stabilizes hip joint

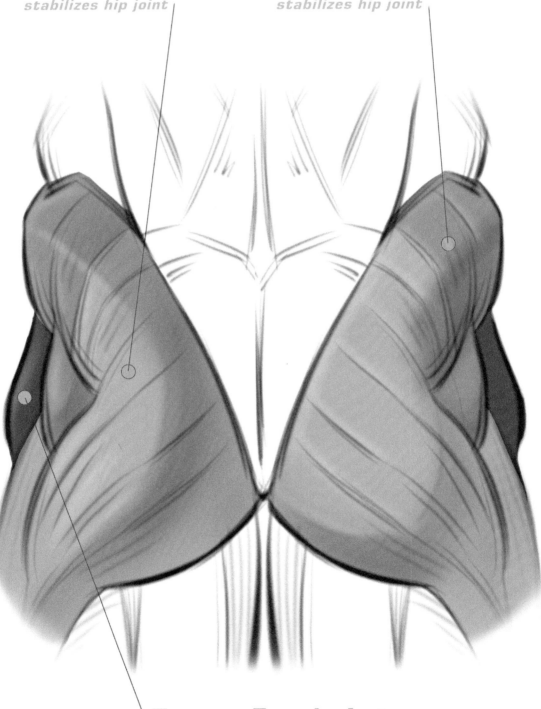

Tensor Fascia Lata
Raises and rotates leg,
stabilizes hip and knee joints

Here in the skeletal, rear view of the pelvis, we can see the sacrum and coccyx bones. The coccyx bone represents the end of the vertebrae train. These two bones create the last FORCE curve of the torso, presented through the curvature of the gluteus maximus.

2

The gluteus maximus muscles contract in the left leg and in the further, right leg. You can still see the wrench shape here in perspective. Notice that the lower end of the glutes sweeps around to the side of the leg to connect to the femur.

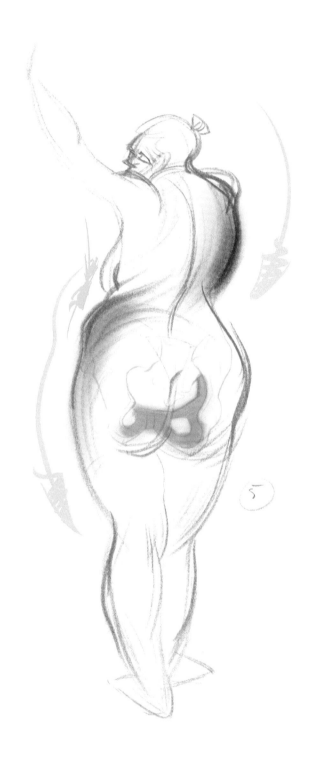

The pelvis again helps define the form of the lower body. Notice the surface lines moving over the lower back and around the left side of the left hip.

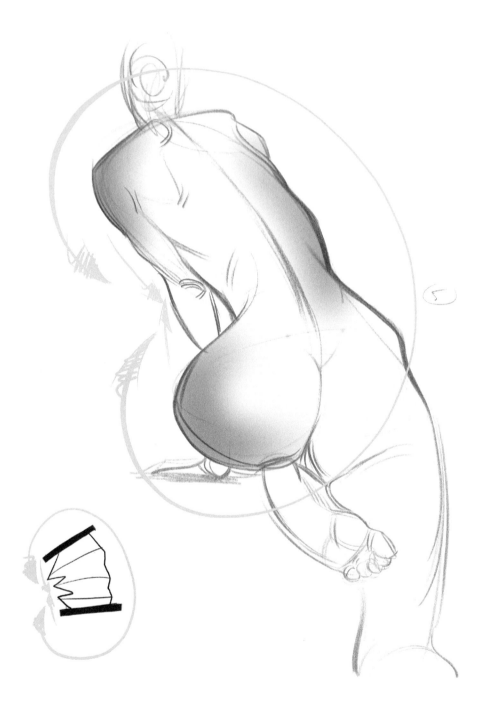

This pose functions like the accordion. Although subtle, I used the structure of the protruding right hip to add believability to the drawing's anatomy. Since the left side is contracted and softer, I did not draw the left hip. The sacral dimples on the lower back of women create an excellent triangular shape that helps create form for the lower back. Notice the last FORCE in the neck that creates a rhythm with the right side of the body.

In this final drawing for this chapter, you can see that the left obliques ride over and around the left hip. Although there are no markings of the specific anatomy, I think about the pelvis as I draw so that all the lines land in the correct locations and create believable, FORCEFUL drawings. The simple moment of overlap I used above the hip gives us quick anatomy and depth.

EXERCISES AND TIPS

1. Make sure that the spine aligns with the center of the rear end.

2. On women, use the sacral dimples to further the clarity of the form of the lower back.

3. The bottom of the glutes sweeps around to the center of the side of the leg.

The four **QUAD**riceps are some of the larger muscles in the body and thus are very powerful. One of the four muscles is hidden underneath the three, so we only draw three of the quadriceps. Imagine the knee as the elbow joint. Therefore, the quadriceps are the triceps of the leg. They raise the lower leg, extending it. The sartorius, the longest muscle in the body, moves across the upper leg, from the iliac crest to the inside of the knee joint, and finally ends on the tibia. Remember that the muscles always move across a joint in order to have function.

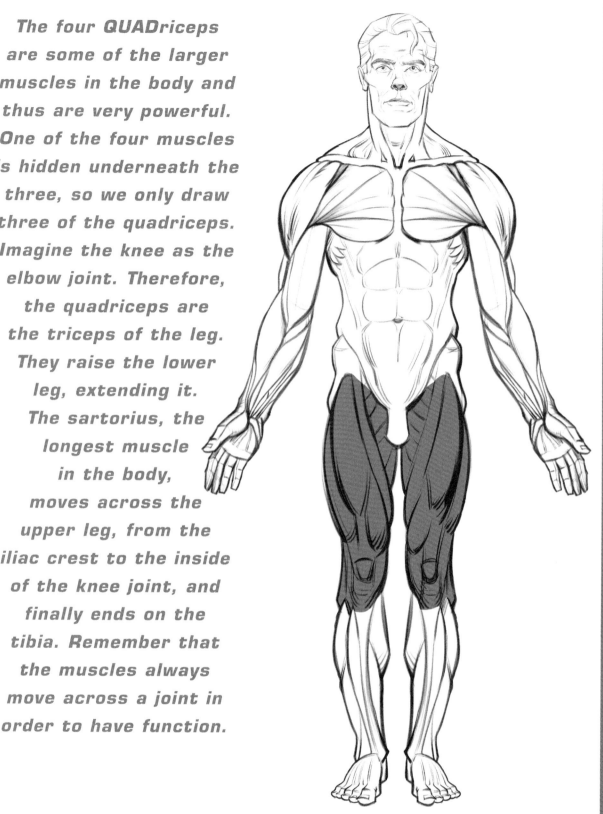

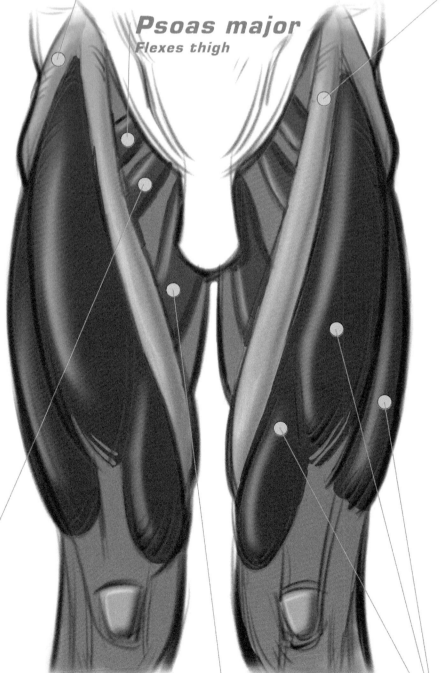

Tensor Fascia Lata
Raises and rotates leg, stabilizes hip and knee joints

Sartorius
Raises and internally rotates leg at the hip joint

Psoas major
Flexes thigh

Pectineus
Helps lift and rotate the thigh

Adductor Longus
Helps lift and rotate the thigh

Quadriceps
Extends leg at knee joint, pulls leg up to body

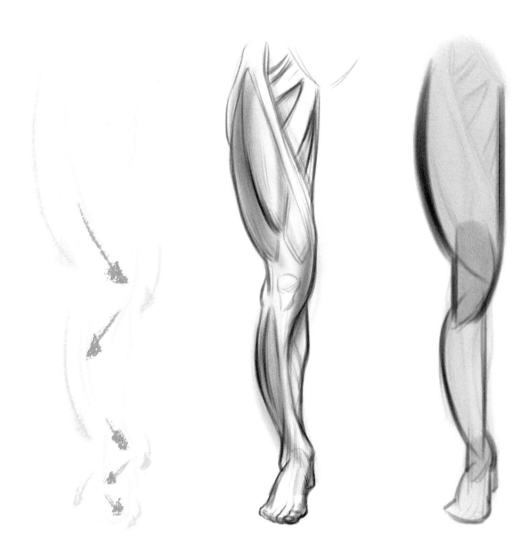

Since we are moving on to the legs, let's look at the rhythms of the entire leg before diving into the thigh region. I call the pattern of FORCE here "outside, inside, outside." This pattern starts with that topmost blue arrow and then moves across the thigh to the inside knee. In the front view, this inside–outside pattern continues all the way down the leg.

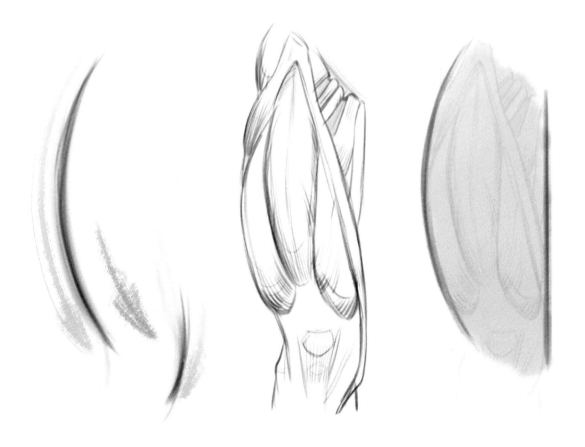

Looking more closely at the thigh, you can see that FORCE applies itself into the inside knee. The sartorius' origin is at the iliac crest, and the insertion resides at the tibia, moving across the knee joint. You will never find DIRECTIONAL FORCE in the inner region of the upper leg or the outer region of the knee.

Starting on the left side of the page, the medical names for the three surface quadriceps are the vastus lateralis, the rectus femoris, and the vastus medialis. The one quadricep muscle that is hidden under the other three is called the vastus intermedius. The origin point for the quadriceps resides at the top of the humerus bone.

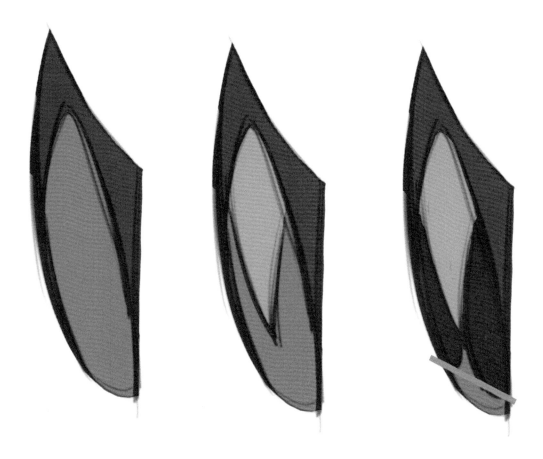

Here is a simple shape process for filling in the anatomy of the front, upper thigh.

The initial shape in the left drawing creates the asymmetry that clarifies how FORCE moves from the outside of the thigh to the inside knee. Then, the second light shape begins the separation of the three quadriceps. Then, the drawing on the right drops in the final two quad shapes. What is integral to notice here is the angle created with the bottom of the two quads and how it directs us to the interior knee.

Here is a foreshortened thigh and the other is parallel to us. Once you know the general flat-shape mapping of the muscle, you can apply that idea to the more simple structures of the body, such as the simple tube of the foreshortened leg. Notice in the original drawing that the importance of placing the iliac crest line into the white space of the body allowed me to connect the sartorius down to the knee and give the body some form.

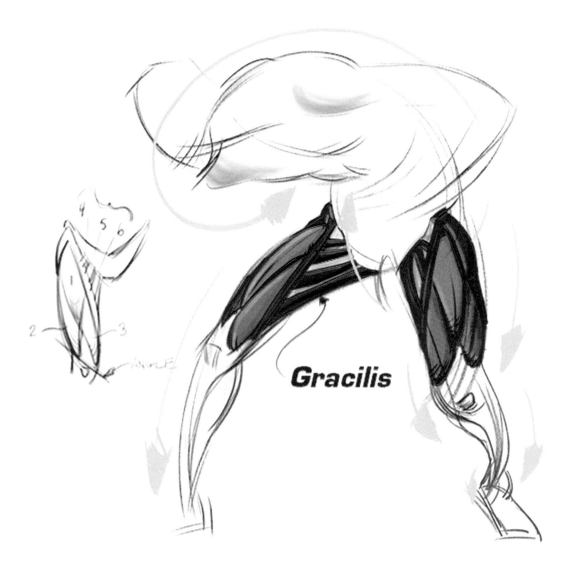

Gracilis

I find it good practice to know the amount of muscles there are within the larger shapes of the body. Here, in the upper thigh, there are three muscles: the quadriceps, in the center surface of the leg (#1–#3) between the tensor fascia lata (TFL) and the sartorius.

The line drawing on the left shows the muscle count for the inner thigh. From the sartorius to the gracilis, which is found at the center of the inner thigh, there are three primary muscles: the psoas major (#4), the pectineus (#5), and the adductor longus (#6).

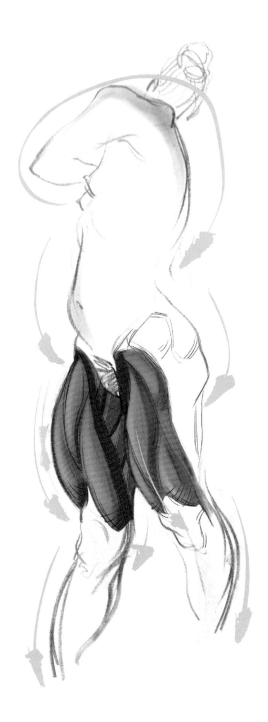

Here, you can see the simplicity of the teardrop shapes of the three quadriceps in each of the thighs. When I started writing this book, I thought that I had found a simple rule that CONTRACTION was always on the opposite side of a Directional FORCE, but, here in the thigh, you can see that both types of FORCES can occur at the same time, so this rule does NOT work.

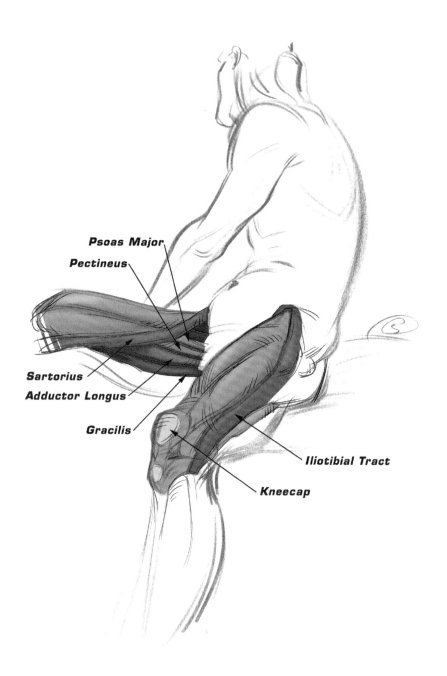

Psoas Major

Pectineus

Sartorius

Adductor Longus

Gracilis

Iliotibial Tract

Kneecap

This drawing shows us the two muscles that create the sides of the quadriceps territories. The far leg shows the sartorius wrapping around the form of the thigh. You can see how the inner shape of the thigh is filled with numerous muscles that I have labeled above. The close leg shows the iliotibial tract, emerging from the TFL.

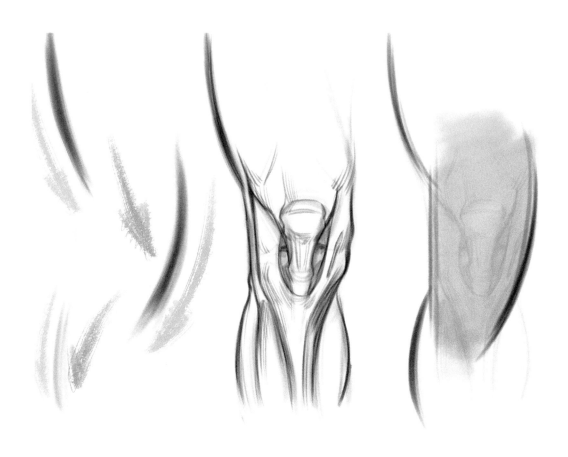

In this close-up of the frontal knee region, you can see how FORCE travels to the inside knee as a bridge to the lower leg. Notice how the shape of the knee is a straight to curve, with the curve on the interior.

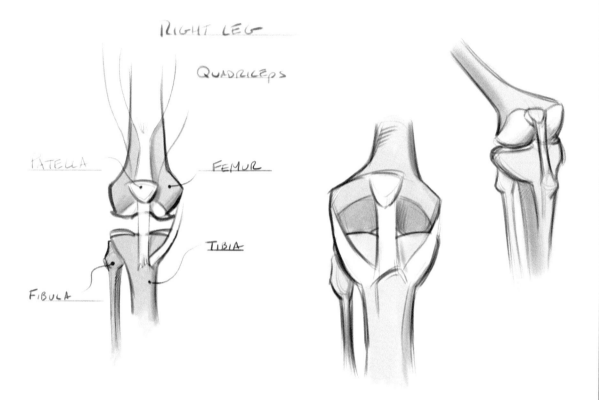

RIGHT LEG

QUADRICEPS

PATELLA

FEMUR

TIBIA

FIBULA

Artists typically find it frustrating to illustrate the knee joint. Above is a simple illustration of the knee and how it bends. I focused for at least a semester in school to grasp drawing the knee. Keep in mind the simplicity of the two major bones, the femur and the tibia, connected by the patella ligament with the patella or the kneecap, itself floating between the two bones.

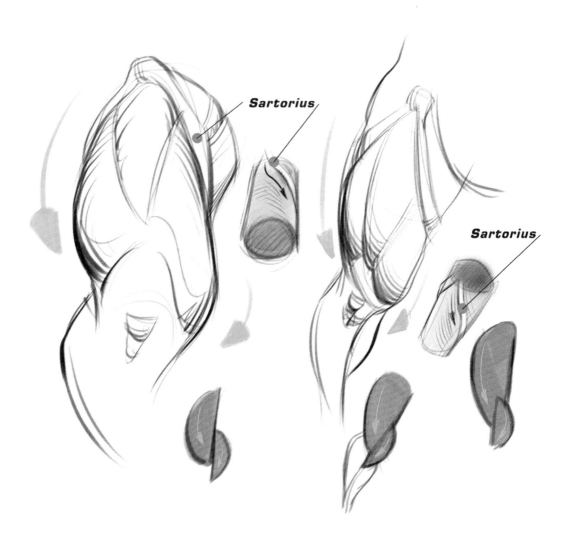

Sartorius

Sartorius

I love using the sartorius to present form in the thigh. Next to each of the leg drawings is a tube in the same orientation as the leg. Over the surface of the tube is the sartorius, showing the wrapping function. Below are three, orange shape diagrams simplifying the rhythm of the leg and the knee.

EXERCISES AND TIPS

1. Use the iliac crest to center the top of the leg in the front view.
2. Find the left and right boundaries of the quadriceps territory by drawing the TFL and the sartorius.
3. Use the sartorius to help present the roundness and form of the thigh.

In the profile, **FORCE** always resides in the front edge or quadricep area of the upper leg. It drives down to the knee and then can move to the front or rear of the lower leg, depending on the function of the leg. The edge of the quadriceps is tucked under the TFL on the side of the leg. In this chapter, we will look at the hamstrings and the quadriceps to further understand their relationship to one another, similar to the biceps and triceps of the arm.

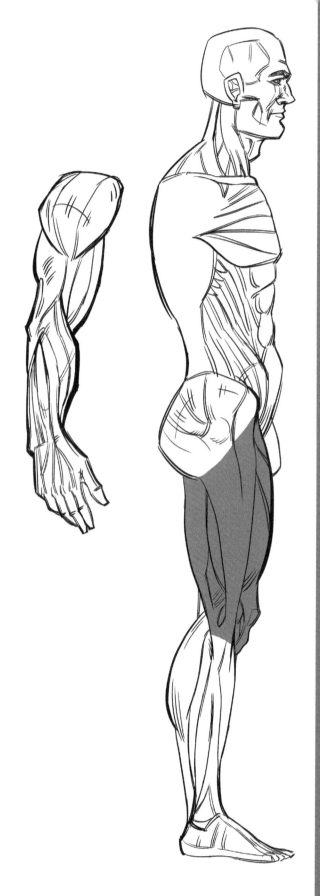

Tensor Fascia Lata
Raises and rotates leg, stabilizes hip and knee joints

Sartorius
Raises and internally rotates leg at the hip joint

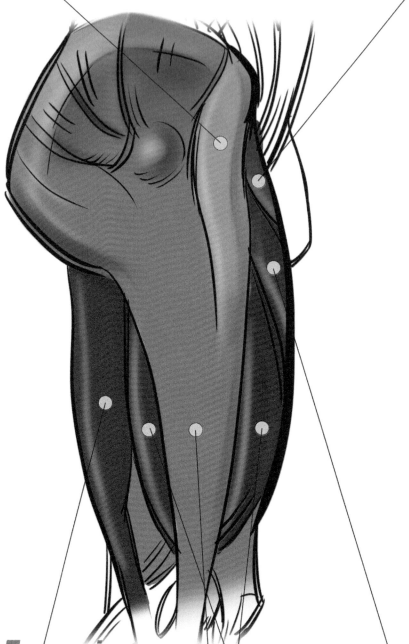

Biceps Femoris
Contracts leg at knee joint, rotates leg outward

Quadriceps
Extends leg at knee joint, pulls leg up to body

Iliotibial Tract
Extension of TFL

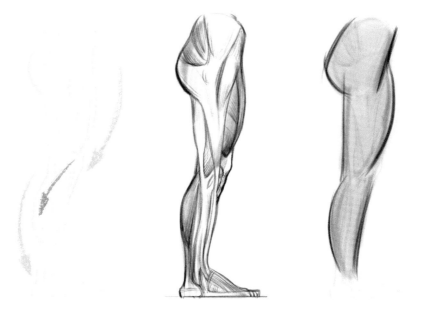

As we did in the prior section, here is the full flow of rhythm down the leg, from the pelvis to the foot. Notice the passing of FORCE from the front of the thigh to the back of the calf through the knee. In the shape filter on the far right, see the straight-to-curve shape flipping from side to side as we move down the leg.

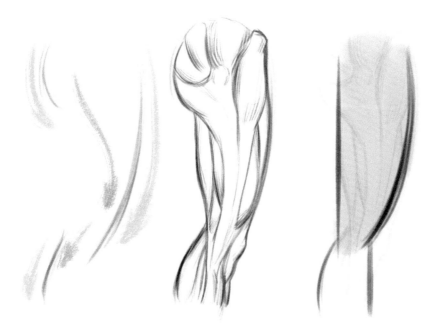

In this close-up version of the side view, you can see how FORCE from the gluteus maximus connects to the front of the thigh.

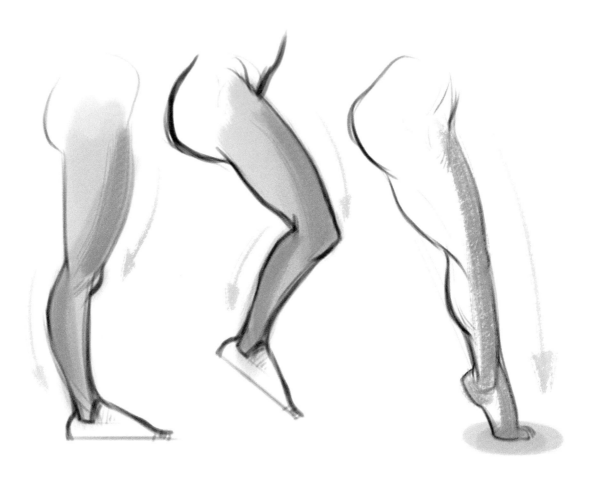

Let's look at the length of the side view of the leg. Typically, FORCE moves through the leg, from the front of the thigh to the back of the calf. The drawing on the far right shows a pose where the FORCE goes through the entire front of the leg down to the ball of the foot.

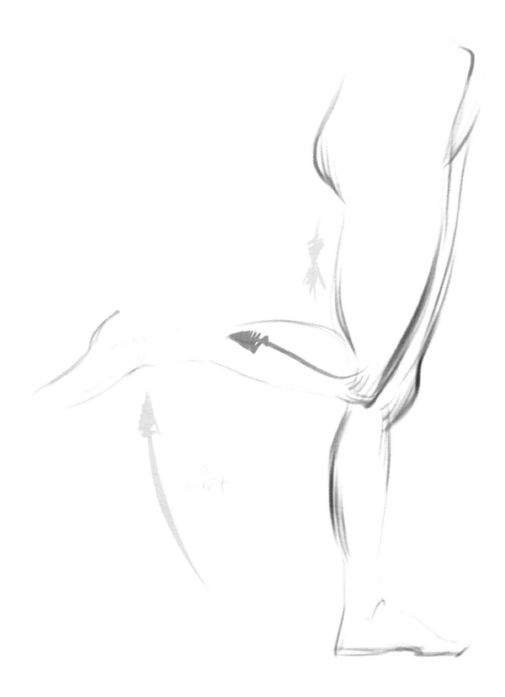

As I mentioned in the earlier section, if you can imagine the knee as the elbow, then the quads are the triceps, which makes the arm biceps the biceps femoris of the leg. The biceps femoris help create the hamstring muscle group found here. The CONTRACTION of the hamstrings lifts the legs up.

2 GLUTES INSIDE WRENCH

○1

○2

OUTSIDE QUAD
MOVES UNDER T.F.L

Notice that the outside quadriceps move under the TFL, the light purple shape. The TFL helps rotate the leg and lift it upward from the front and side angles of the figure. The two smaller images on the side show the shape and form of the leg and how, when simplified, it is once more a straight-to-curve design.

Notice how the pelvis connects to the leg and how the iliotibial tract, colored light purple, travels down the side of the leg until it reaches the tibia, as seen above in the lightest tone. Remember that what makes the muscular system work is the muscles moving across joints.

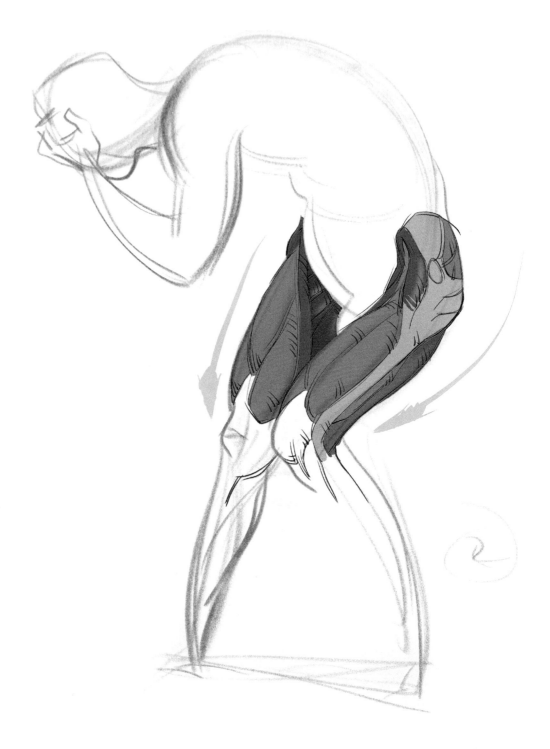

FORCE drives down the outside of the thighs to push the knees together in this pose of anguish.

EXERCISES AND TIPS

1. Use the front edge of the TFL to cut down the center of the leg.

2. Practice seeing the different ways that FORCE can travel through the knee.

3. Do NOT create symmetry in the upper leg in this view. The curve of the hamstring or the rear muscles of the leg is shorter than the quadriceps of the front.

When it comes to the back of the leg, the rhythm of **FORCES** is the same as those found in the front view, the outside thigh, the inside knee, and the outside calf. The hamstrings, consisting of three muscles that I have filtered down to the two most prominent, are centered in the back view, from under the glutes to the knee where they separate and wrap around the outsides of the knee.

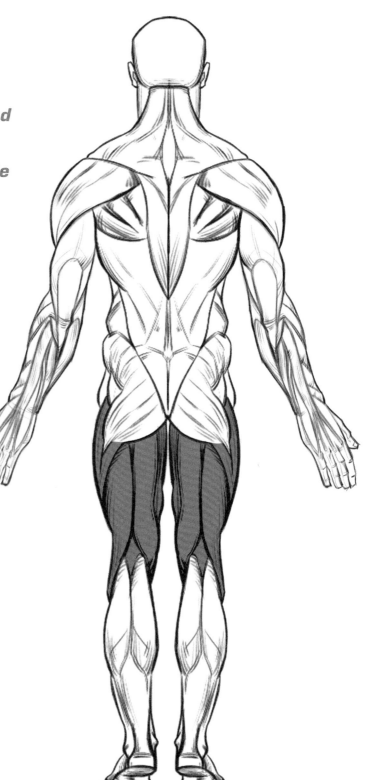

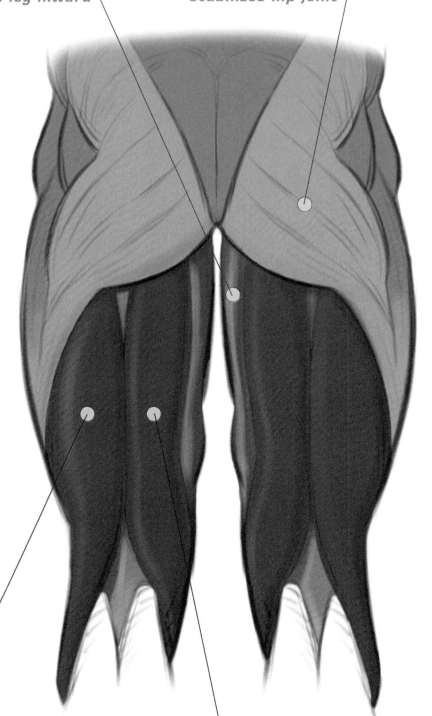

Gracilis
**Pulls leg toward center,
rotates leg inward**

Gluteus Maximus
**Helps raise leg on side and rear,
stabilizes hip joint**

Biceps Femoris
**Contracts leg at knee joint,
rotates leg outward**

Semitendinosus
**Contracts leg at knee joint,
rotates leg inward**

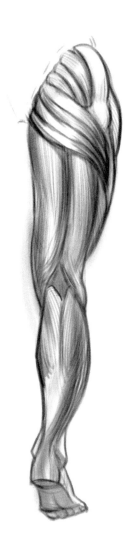

Finally, in this last view of the upper leg, you can see how the rhythms are the same as they are in the front view. The musculature of the back of the leg is divided in half. The halves, the biceps femoris and the semitendinosus, are more commonly known as the hamstrings.

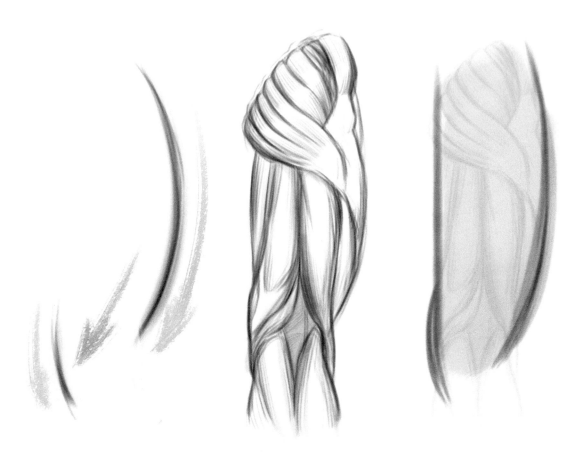

Here is a closer view of the upper-right leg, and you can see the back of the knee and how the calves sweep out from underneath the hamstrings. The FORCES once more show how they move across the knee, from the outside thigh to the inside knee.

The top of the calf muscles or their origins, start at the bottom of the femur and move across the back of the knee joint where their insertion points land on the tibia and fibula.

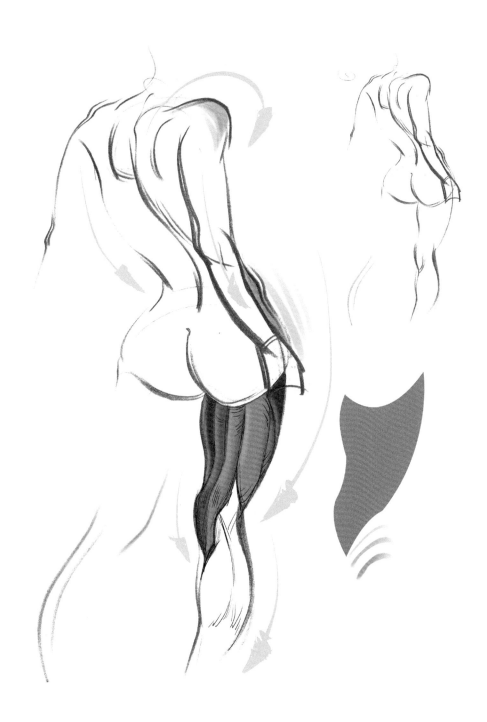

Here, we can see how FORCE bounces down the leg. To the right are the FORCE shapes of the thigh. The shape follows all of the FORCEFUL rules. I threw some purple arcs under the shape to show the form of the lower leg.

This drawing is from my imagination, and it uses all of the FORCES that I have shown you in this chapter and how the anatomical leg-centering concept works between the hamstrings in the upper leg and the calves in the lower leg.

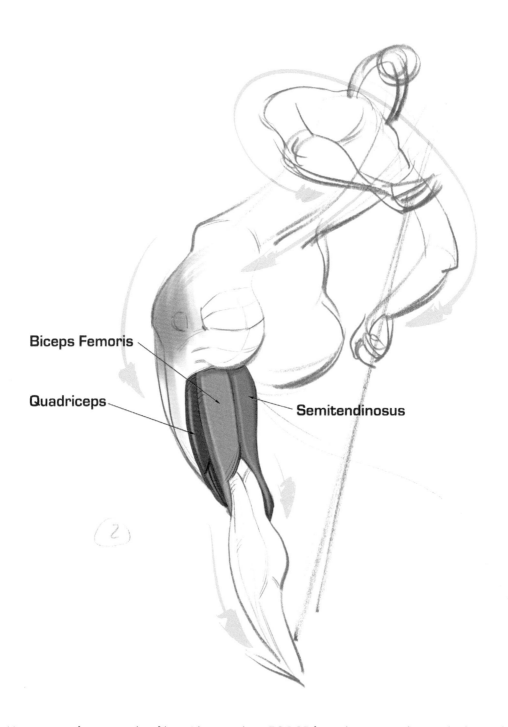

Biceps Femoris

Quadriceps

Semitendinosus

Here is a perfect example of how I love to drive FORCE from the torso right into the hip. It then travels down the strong leg. Remember that the biceps femoris and the semitendinosus are two muscles that create the hamstring group. The third muscle is the semimembranosus, not illustrated above. It lies closest to the interior of the thigh and quite frankly is never seen in the figure.

I end the upper leg section with a drawing that shows the simple rhythm of the right leg and then how anatomy develops efficient shapes in the left leg. Notice the overarching curve of FORCE from the pelvis to the ankle.

EXERCISES AND TIPS

1. Use the centering rule to remember the anatomy of the leg's back view.

2. If you can remember the rhythms of the leg in the front view, then you have remembered them for the back view. Practice the outside, inside, outside pattern.

3. Keep in mind that FORCE moves from the outside of the thigh to the inside of the knee.

In this view, we can best see the natural curvature of the tibia. This curve drives **FORCE** from the outside calf edge right into the inside ankle. The lower leg has two bones, similar to the forearm. Here, though, they do not help in rotating the lower leg as they do in rotating the forearm because the wrist and ankle joints are constructed differently. The tibialis anterior is one of the major muscles found here, and when it contracts, it raises the top of the foot upward, toward the shin. The foot bears all of our weight and needs strength and flexibility to allow us the actions of walking, jumping, and running.

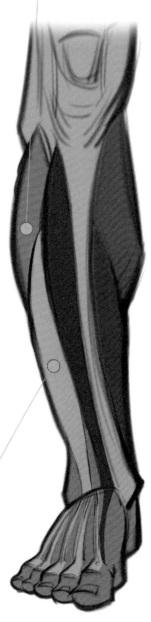
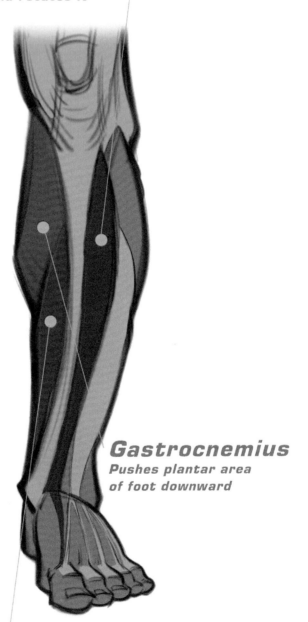

Peroneus Longus
Plantar flexes the foot and helps support foot arch

Tibialis Anterior
Raises top of foot upward and rotates it

Gastrocnemius
Pushes plantar area of foot downward

Extensor Digitorum
Raises top of foot upward

Soleus
Pushes tip of foot downward

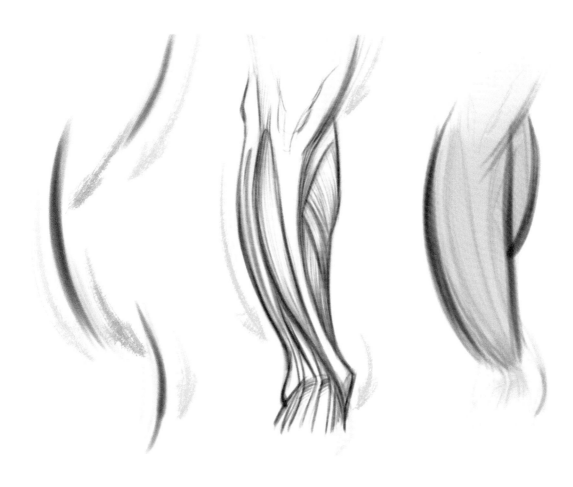

The front view of the calf shows that FORCE now moves through the knee to the outside of the calf and to the inside of the ankle. The tibia defines the inside area of the ankle. You will never find DIRECTIONAL FORCE in the inside calf region of the lower leg.

In the shape filter, you can see the major straight-to-curve shape. The addition of the smaller straight-to-curve shape creates a more organic representation of the calf's silhouette.

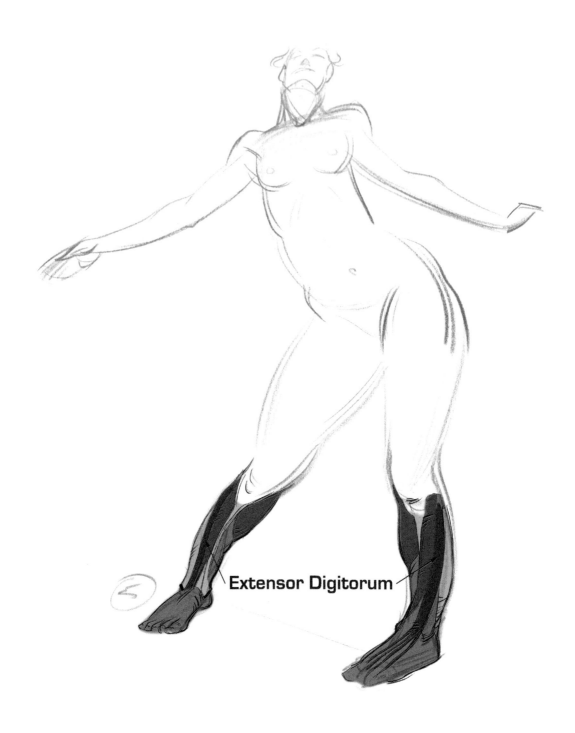

Extensor Digitorum

Yes, there is an extensor digitorum in the calves, as well as the forearms. The extensor digitorum divides and moves down to each of the toes of the foot, except for the big toe. This muscle helps raise the top of the foot upward.

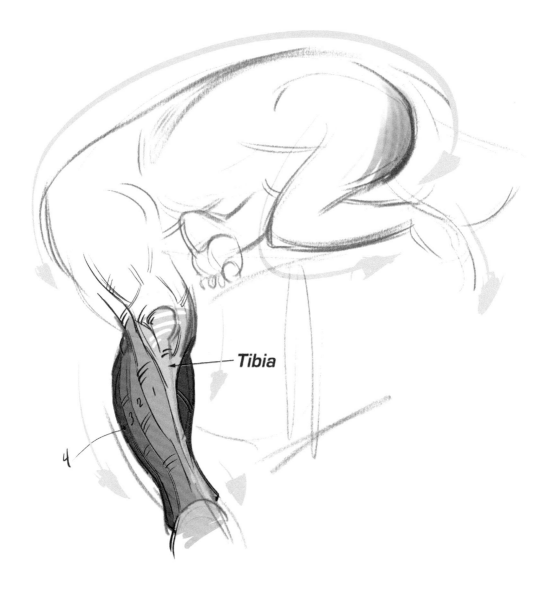

Tibia

As we move around the side of the leg, away from the tibia, there are four muscles until we reach the calf muscles in the rear:

1. *Tibialis anterior*—This muscle runs along the length of the tibia.

2. *Extensor digitorum*—When contracted, raises the top of the foot.

3. *Fibularis longus*—Runs along the length of the fibula.

4. *Soleus*—The last muscle before we get to the calf muscles in the back of the lower leg. This muscle is similar to the brachialis in the upper arm, sandwiched between the calf muscles and the tibia, presenting itself on both the outside and inside of the lower leg.

FOOT—FRONT VIEW

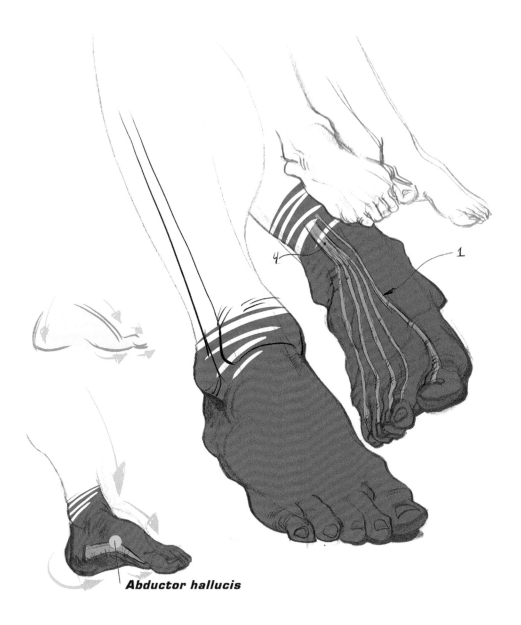

Abductor hallucis

In these more intense drawings of the feet, we can see the four tendons from the extensor digitorum, labeled "4," running over the top of the foot. The single tendon, labeled "1," runs to the big toe and comes from the extensor hallucis longus.

The green muscle in the bottom-left drawing is called the abductor hallucis. It allows you to point your big toe downward since contracting this region of the foot shortens its distance.

I drew the side view of the foot here to show you how it functions relative to the front.

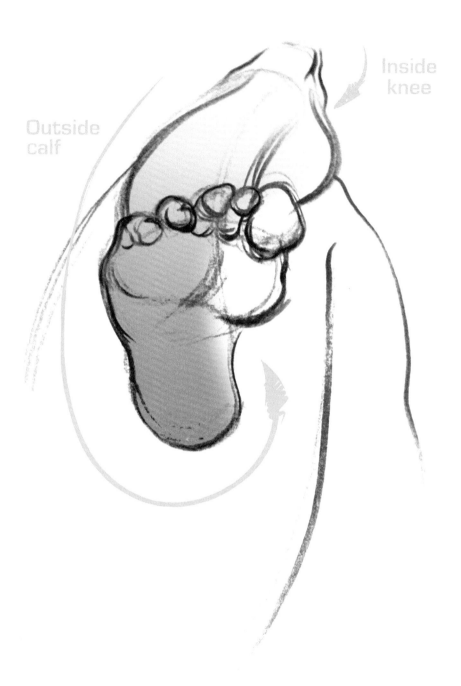

Outside
calf

Inside
knee

No matter what angle you see the front of the lower leg, the rhythm is still "inside knee to outside calf." The orange region not only shows the APPLIED FORCE but also that I thought through the foot, and made it transparent in my mind, to connect the calf to the bottom of the foot.

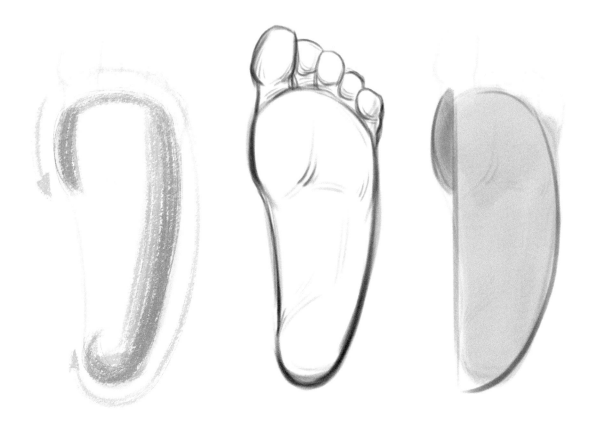

Believe it or not, even the bottom of the foot is composed of FORCEFUL shapes. Most of the FORCE runs along the outside edge of the foot and then into the ball of the foot, basically surrounding the foot's arch.

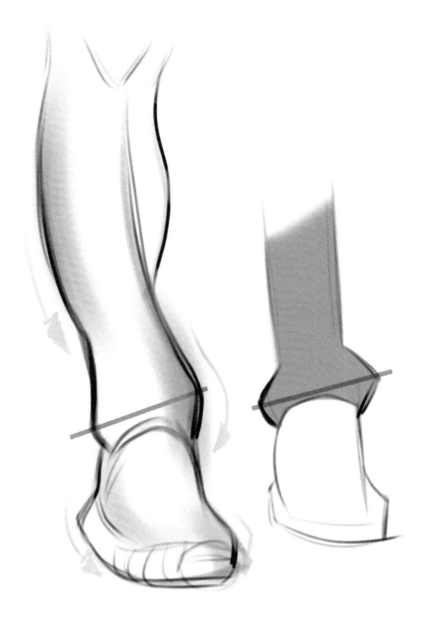

Similar to the "wrench" shape that we saw in the pelvis and the side of the upper leg, we have that once more in the front view of the ankle. When I draw the connection of the lower leg to the foot, I think about all of the body's weight pushing down on the ankle and dispersing down onto the foot. Notice the angle of the inside and outside bones of the ankle.

See the loop over the top of the foot? This is a crucial line that I use to define the perspective angle of the foot and therefore the lower leg.

The top-left drawing shows how FORCE travels into the ball of the foot and then into the toes. The other drawing shows the EXTENSOR DIGITORUM BREVIS of the foot. These muscles are split into four and are connected to all the toes, except the pinky, to help raise them up toward the front of the leg.

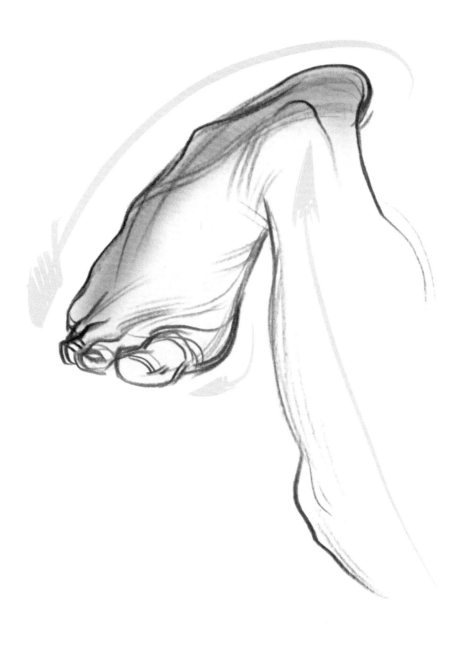

FORCE drives upward along the outside of the calf to the heel of the foot and then plunges down the outside edge to the ball of the foot. Here, all the FORCE pushes down onto the ground and out the toes.

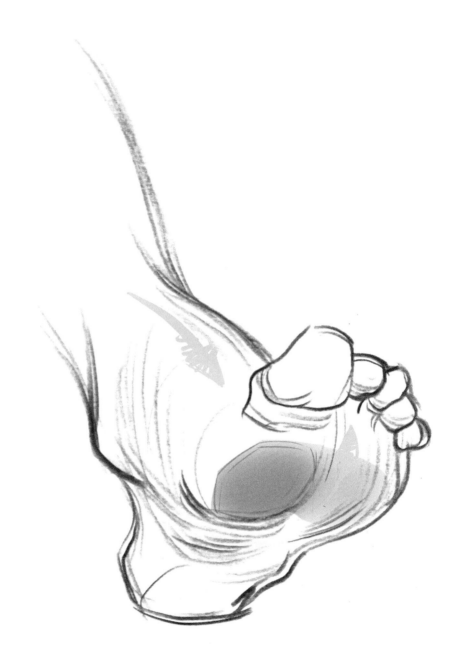

When thinking about FORCE's travels, think through the figure, as seen here with the FORCE of the calf driving once more down to the ball of the foot.

EXERCISES AND TIPS

1. Whew, drawing lower legs and feet. It is best to practice a lot here. Draw YOUR feet often. Think about FORCE driving down from the lower leg to the foot.

2. It is great to have a mirror on the ground, like they do at shoe stores. This gives you the opportunity to draw your feet from numerous angles.

3. Use the curve at the top of the foot where it meets the lower leg to define the perspective angle of the lower leg.

In the profile, you can clearly see how the **CONTRACTION** of the calf muscles helps push the ball of the foot downward, pivoted at the ankle joint. These regions of the muscles are strong, carrying around our weight all day as we walk, jump, and run. There are primarily two types of calf muscle: (1) long and (2) short. In the side view we can also better understand the design and structure of the shoes we wear due to **FORCE**.

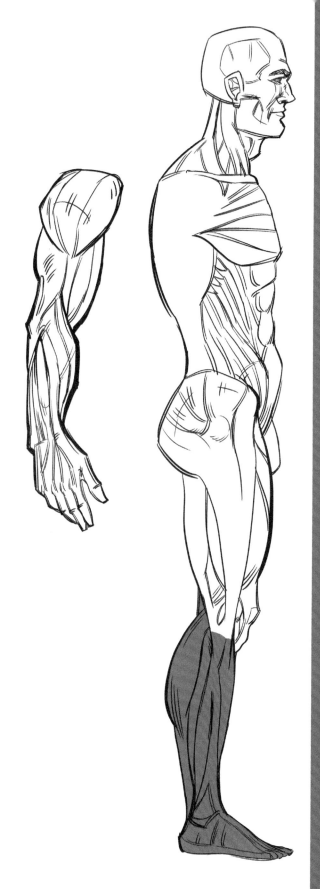

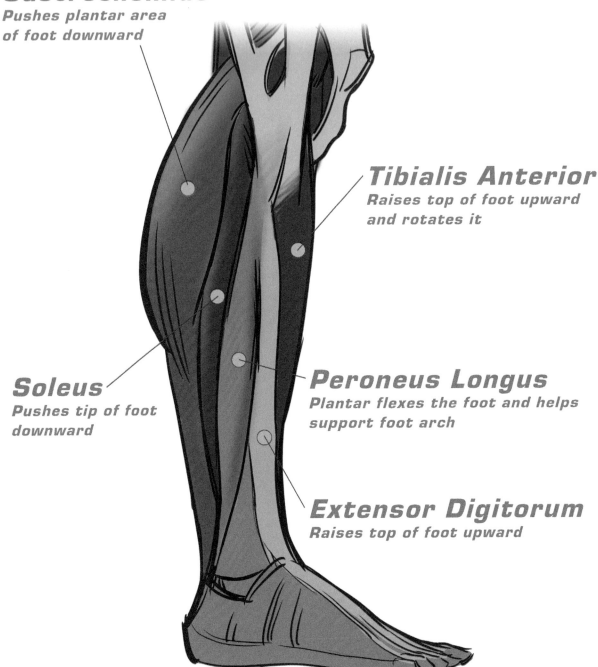

Gastrocnemius
Pushes plantar area
of foot downward

Tibialis Anterior
Raises top of foot upward
and rotates it

Soleus
Pushes tip of foot
downward

Peroneus Longus
Plantar flexes the foot and helps
support foot arch

Extensor Digitorum
Raises top of foot upward

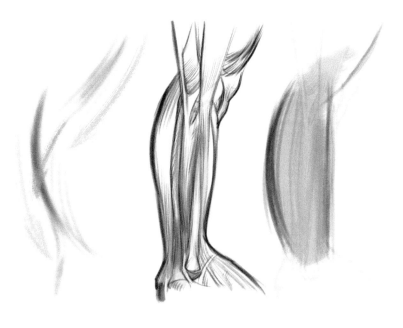

The rhythm in the calf region of the leg moves from the front of the thigh to the back of the calf. You can see the line art of the anatomy and then the simple FORCE shapes in the far right image.

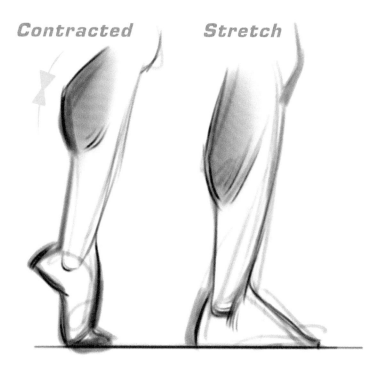

Contracted   *Stretch*

The calf muscles contract, thus pushing the leg upward and the ball of the foot downward, allowing the foot to balance on the ball area.

So here is a side view of the lower calf in a pose where the model stretches her foot outward, away from the body:

1. Gastrocnemius

2. Soleus

3. Fibularis longus

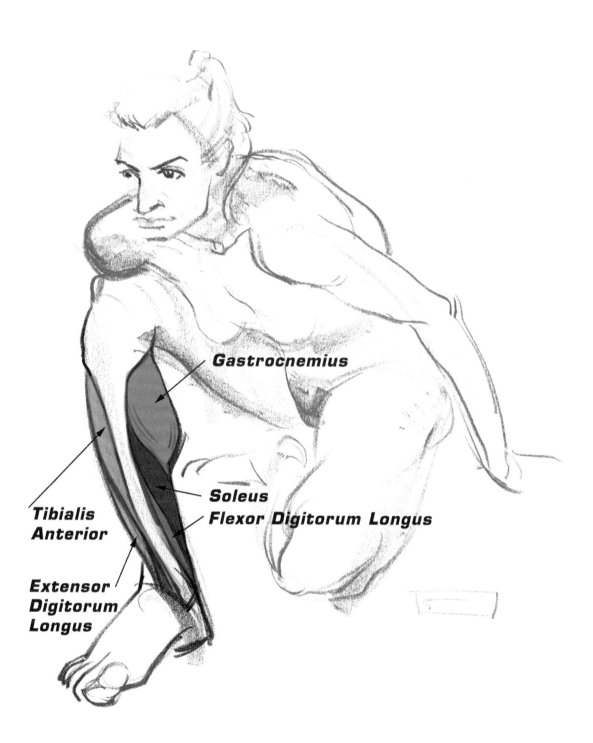

Gastrocnemius

Soleus
Flexor Digitorum Longus

Tibialis
Anterior

Extensor
Digitorum
Longus

The structure of the leg is used as a triangular support to the weight of the body. When I say triangular, I mean the triangle shape that is created by the two angles of the upper and lower leg and then the floor.

FOOT—OUTSIDE AND INSIDE VIEWS

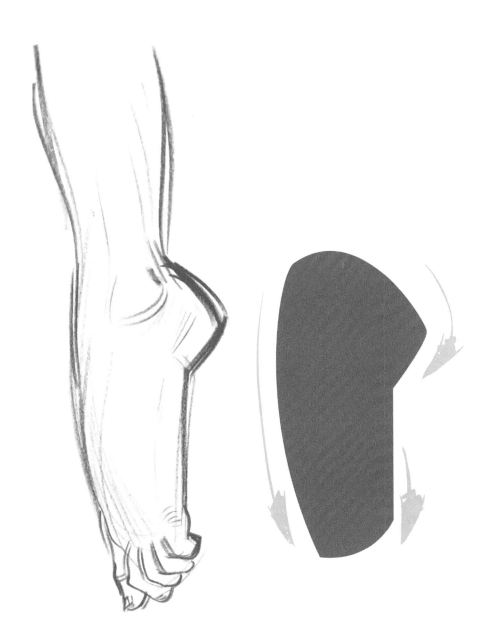

Here is the simplified shape that I saw when drawing this more complex-looking drawing. Notice how FORCE drives over the top of the foot into the toe region.

Here, the rhythms are aggressive and quickly thrust down the leg to the ball of the foot as the model extends his foot outward. This again is due to the CONTRACTION of the calf muscles and those on the top of the foot.

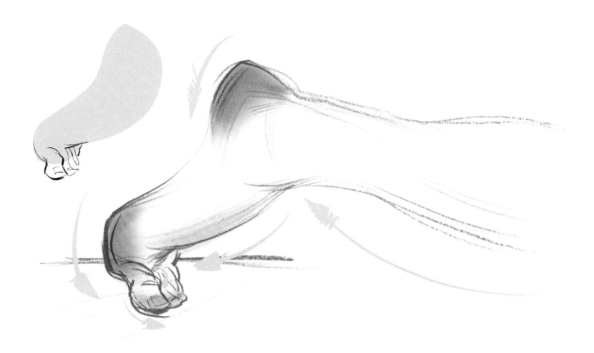

This pose presents a very different operation. Here, the ball of the foot is stretching out, and the toes are dragging on the model stand, compressed under the weight of the leg.

EXERCISES AND TIPS

1. Try raising your body on your toes and feel the calves contract to lift your heels up off of the ground. Feel the strain in your feet.

2. When drawing the foot in the side view, keep in mind the arch of the foot on the interior surface.

3. Try to notice the unique qualities of the models you draw and the feet you conjure from imagination.

Here we are at the last anatomy chapter of the book, the back of the lower leg. Once more, we can see natural centers prevalent down the middle of the calves. The "calves" is a name given to all the muscles in this region and view of the lower leg. The calves' tendon is the famous Achilles tendon. The muscles in the rear view of the lower leg move across two joints, the knee and ankle!

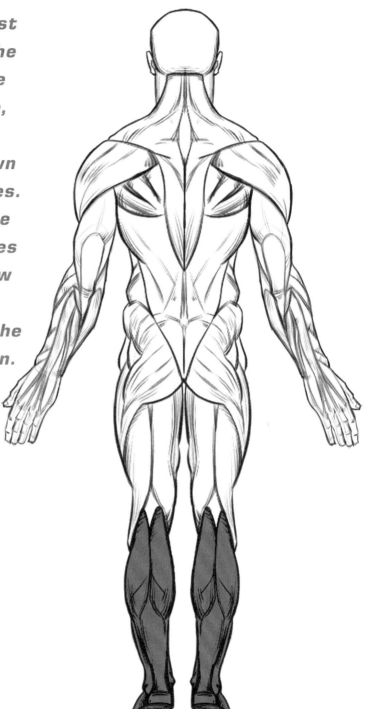

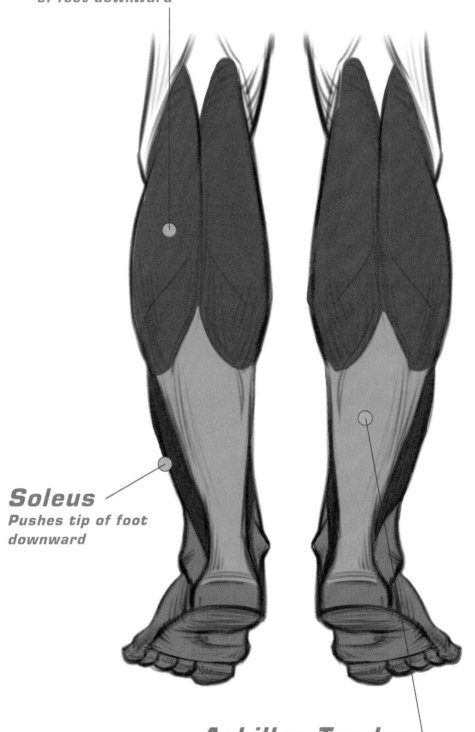

Gastrocnemius
*Pushes plantar area
of foot downward*

Soleus
*Pushes tip of foot
downward*

Achilles Tendon
Contracts to push tip of foot down

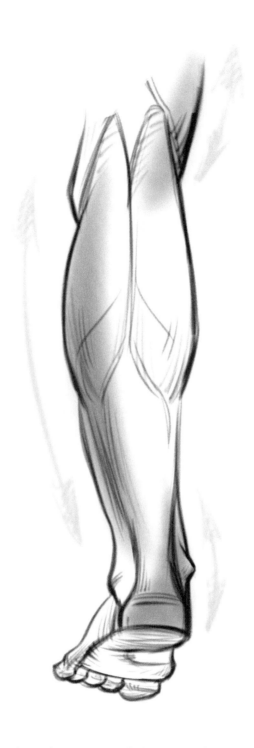

Our "inside, outside" pattern, shown here, starts with the inside of the knee, then the outside of the calf, and ends on the inside of the ankle.

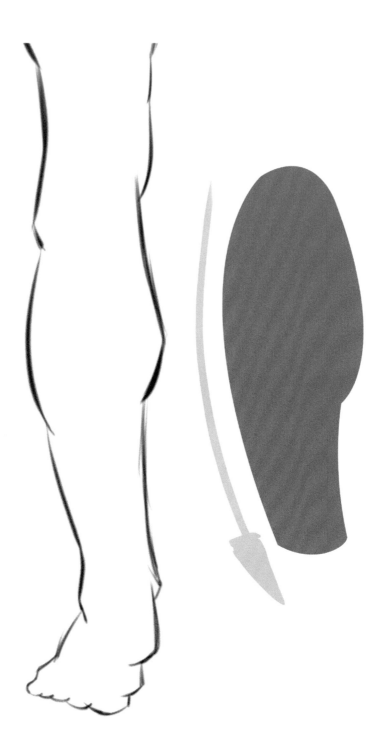

As you are drawing the calf, keep in mind its shape. As mentioned in Chapter 3, you want to evade the blasphemous egg. Evasion occurs through the asymmetrical shape silhouette, as seen above.

Outside

Outside

Inside

Front

Back

The back of the lower leg is pretty simple. Keep in mind how the calf muscles connect from the Achilles tendon down to the heel of the foot.

Here, we can see how the CONTRACTION of the calf muscles (gastrocnemius) allows the heel of the foot to raise off the ground. This shortening of the muscles pivots on the ankle and drives the foot into the ground.

This last drawing shows the left, lower leg parallel to the camera and the right, lower leg oriented with tight foreshortening. FORCE flows through rhythms to connect these areas of the leg to the rest of the figure.

EXERCISES AND TIPS

1. Remember centering and that the inside calf muscle is slightly shorter than the outside. You want to drive FORCE down the outside edge of the calf.

2. Keep connecting the outside edge to the inside of the ankle.

3. Keep in mind that asymmetry will save you from the "blasphemous egg" shape that is easy to fall into for the calf region of the leg.

Chapter 13
Closing Thoughts

I hope that you have enjoyed our anatomical journey together through the theory of FORCE! We have learned how all of the interwoven muscles of the human body work as a perfect system.

We are quite amazing machines in terms of function and design. Every muscle resides exactly where it belongs to allow us to perform an amazing range of motions.

Stay curious, intrigued, and eager to learn.

Practice, nothing beats it! Do it with conviction and fail often. Get up and learn more. You can do it; I promise.

Please feel free to reach out to me at mike@drawingforce.com.

I would love to hear from you.

Sincerely,
Mike Mattesi

Index